GW00455915

FAIL-PROOF GUIDE TO BACKYARD CHICKENS

Discover the Secrets of Raising Chickens for
Fun, Profit, and Sustainable Living...
Even If You've Never Owned a Chicken

ALVYNA CHARLOTTE

Table of Contents

INTRODUCTION

"I began raising chickens primarily for their eggs, but over the years, I've also grown fond of caring for them and learning about their many different breeds and varieties," Martha Stewart (US Entertainer, n.d).

There is a certain charm to raising chickens, enjoying the bounty of their eggs and even making a special meal from their succulent bodies. In a world where everything is mass-produced, natural farming methods are becoming something of a hype, and people relish the idea of being able to produce their own organically raised poultry and eggs.

Yet this can be a daunting prospect for most of us, having never had the experience of living on a farm. Chickens have their own sets of problems, diseases, requirements, and challenges for successful management in the urban environment. However, with a little help, it may be easier than you believed possible.

Being an effective and successful chicken keeper requires some planning, a slight shift in your mindset, and the knowledge offered in this book. This will allow you to make informed decisions from the get-go like: choosing a bird type that suits your climate and your needs, creating a suitable environment for your chickens, knowing what to do with the eggs, how to raise healthy chicks, and what to do with the mountains of poop that they will make. You will even learn how to think like a chicken and understand their unique behavior to better enjoy them.

As with anything in life, there are pros and cons to raising chickens in your backyard. It may seem charming to have a rooster crowing at three o'clock in the morning, but your neighbors may find it less so (not to mention that it may be illegal to keep roosters in an urban area according to your city bylaws). If you are not careful in ensuring their safety, you may wake up to horror in your backyard when the neighborhood cat decides to embark on a midnight feast. This means that you will need to plan effective ways to keep not only your chickens, but also your neighbors happy. However, the benefits of keeping chickens still outweigh the cons.

They are easy on the eyes, and no one can deny that there is something earthy and heartwarming about seeing a hen with her clutch marching across your yard. Gathering fresh eggs with that rich farm taste when you want, and feeding a whole chattering of feathery bundles that flock around you is certainly entertaining and fun for your children. The varieties that chickens come in are not only diverse, but can even become a passion with many chicken breeders exchanging unique specimens and even a range of chicken competitions being hosted Nationwide.

As pets, chickens also offer charm, and a little known fact is that chickens can become very tame and sociable with their human keepers. They enjoy being stroked and tend to follow people around, hoping for a choice morsel. In their backyard environment, they can help limit insects by eating worms, larvae, and locusts etc., thereby keeping your environment naturally pest-free. Their manure is also a very rich fertilizer that can be used in vegetable gardens, and to green up your lawn. They can even be considered a security measure, as chickens tend to start warning those around them when an intruder enters their domain. Finally, due to their prolific ability to lay eggs and hatch chicks, they can also become a steady source of income with eggs available to sell, and mature birds to slaughter for the table. For your kids, this may be an excellent way to supplement their pocket money and learn about business.

I am definitely the right person to teach you the basics of backyard chicken keeping, having grown up on a farm and turned to raise chickens in my backyard in suburbia. I love chickens, and wanted to ensure that my children have a taste of the wonderful life with farm animals that I had as a child. In this book, I offer you the wealth of my personal knowledge and experience to the new chicken keeper. By the end of this book, you'll be equipped with the skills, knowledge, and mindset involved in keeping chickens in your backyard.

Chickens come in a variety of colors, patterns, shapes, sizes, personalities, and range in their abilities to lay eggs, raise chicks, offer better quality meat and tenacity to adverse weather conditions. They have a social dynamic that should be considered when raising healthy and happy chickens. Image: Annie Theby on Unsplash.

As A Token
of My Gratitude...
Get this FREE guide now!

When it comes to sustainability there is a balance. Most people want to do more to live an eco-friendly life, but they also want to make sure that it doesn't consume all of their time, energy, and money.

So how do you know where that balance is? How do you know if you're doing as much as you can do without dramatically changing the way you live your life?

Are You Ready to Take Sustainability to the Next Level?

Are You Ready for a Change?

Are You Looking to Feel More Fulfilled, Rewarded, and Engaged?

If you answered yes to any of these questions then you're ready to take sustainability to the next level. Don't worry; you don't have to go off the grid if you don't want to. Download this free book and you'll learn 8 different ideas to add more sustainable habits and projects to your life. Choose one or all eight – it's up to you. Visit the link below to download:

https://selfempowermentteam.com/sustainable-living

CHAPTER 1

Why Chickens?

My first business deal was with my mother. I invested in chickens. I sold the eggs to my mother.
-Joel McCrea (US actor) (n.d.).

C hickens are found all over the world in a variety of shapes and sizes. They easily adapt to new environments and offer a range of possibilities to their owners, from being kept as pets to becoming a steady source of income. The reasons for chicken keeping are as diverse as the people who keep chickens. They certainly have more benefits than negatives in their keeping, and once you begin it will be hard to look back and not feel satisfied with your feathered backyard flock.

Why People Keep Chickens

Having an available daily stock of fresh eggs is something that many cooking enthusiasts can only dream of. There is something about freshly laid eggs that is just unique. They taste better, last longer, and are way more nutritious for you. Image: Daniel Tuttle on Unsplash.

Jenny McGruther (2018), a well-known food specialist and holistic nutritionist, has some interesting insights into why people should keep chickens. In most counties across the U.S. there are certain laws to adhere to when keeping chickens, and one of the most common is that the chickens should be hens and forbid the keeping of roosters. The obvious three A.M. crowing may be one of the main reasons for this law. But hens are definitely more valuable in keeping, in any case, unless you specifically want chicks. So here are some of the main reasons to keep chickens (or hens):

- **Eggs**

Fresh eggs are simply that. Fresh. They taste better, and given that you know just what your hens have been eating, you know exactly what you end up eating. Since you can also be assured that they are laid in the natural time cycle (about one egg every 25 hours), you know that you will be getting quality and size. For those of us who love cooking or baking, this will be a blessing, as large eggs will be consistent for the most part.

In commercial chicken farming, most hens are kept in a battery system, where they are caged, have limited mobility (if any) and are fed sometimes questionable foods to increase the production of eggs. At such battery farms, the lights are, for instance, set on a timer to fool the hens into thinking that two days have passed, instead of one, and as a result, they will then lay more than one egg every 25 hours. There is also an increased awareness of the introduction of growth hormones and other chemicals to influence the color of commercially produced eggs. If we are what we eat, then what will this end up doing to us? In the long run, having fresh eggs may not only be about taste, but also about health.

For a steady supply of eggs, you can calculate how many hens to keep, bearing in mind that not all your hens will necessarily begin laying at the same time. If a hen lays an egg once a day, then you would keep six hens should you need a half-dozen eggs daily. If you decide to keep a surplus of eggs, it is a good idea to write the lay-date on each egg that you store. But more on eggs later…

- **Healthier Food Sources**

Many of us consume both eggs and chicken as a food source, and this may at times not be the healthiest option given that commercially kept chickens live in environments that are ill-suited to producing healthy animals. Factory farms feed their chickens on corn, cottonseed, and soy–all grown as GMO (Genetically Modified Organism) crops. This means that the meat or eggs that you buy in a store may not be beneficial to your health. Organically reared animals and free-range eggs are certainly healthier, yet products claiming to be GMO-free are at times suspect, as everything from the fertilizers used to the pest control policies of that particular farm, may influence the so-called natural state of its produce.

Raising your own chickens and using their eggs can offer you a real way to ensure that your family only gets the very best nutrition. Freshly laid organic eggs are quite expensive to buy at farmers' markets, but you can have your own hens produce equally delicious and nutritious eggs at a fraction of the cost; in fact, it will only cost you the price of your organically certified chicken pellets. Leonard (2015) believes that backyard eggs contain more vitamin A and E, and Beta Carotene than battery eggs do, while free-range eggs contain 292mg Omega 3 versus only 0.033mg in battery eggs. These statistics certainly make free-range or backyard eggs a much better option than those tasteless battery eggs that you can buy at any local grocery store.

- **Teaching Your Family About Food**

Anyone who has spent some time around kids will be able to attest to the fact that most children have no clue where their food comes from. If you were to ask them where KFC comes from, they would say, "From the shop," and most of these kids would be absolutely surprised (and perhaps even a little disgusted) to know that chickens come from eggs, and that eggs are laid by hens. If this is a life-view that persists, then it will be no surprise that children grow into adults who have no respect for or knowledge of food.

Keeping chickens allows for your family to build a deeper understanding of their role within the animal kingdom (yes, for all of our brainpower, we are still animals), and allow them to interact and influence the animals in their care. You may see the utter surprise on your child's face the first time that they collect a freshly laid egg and realize that it is warm and still a little soft-shelled as it rests in their hands. Being made responsible for feeding and cleaning after the chickens is also a great way to teach kids about responsibility and the fruits of their labor. Many farmers have taught their kids about food and responsible wealth management by letting them sell eggs, raise chickens for slaughter, and understanding the basic principle of expenses versus income. By raising backyard chickens this is something that you can also do.

Chickens are omnivores and eat anything from the commercially available poultry feeds, maize crush, and garden bugs, to fruits and vegetables from your kitchen. Image: Arisa Chattasa on Unsplash.

- **Chickens are Convenient to Care for**

After the initial time and money lay-out of getting chickens, building a safe area for them to move around in (or planning to let them free-range), and constructing a suitable coop, the actual time that they will require for maintenance is very little. It takes less than ten minutes a day to water and feed them, and perhaps lock them up safely at night to ward off the prowling neighborhood cat. As a bonus, free-range chickens tend to fertilize your garden on their own, reducing the frequency with which you need to clean the coup area.

Feed wise, they require very little, and you can supplement their poultry pellets or maize crush with safe kitchen scraps, thereby helping with recycling natural waste materials from your home. Most chicken feed is also relatively inexpensive when compared to dog food, for instance. For the most part, your chickens will be quite happy to scratch away and eat whatever is available, and it's simply up to you to ensure that they have enough food and water available. They eat all day long, so you don't have to keep mealtimes but don't be surprised if they do tend to hang around the kitchen door when you start cooking supper.

- **Bye-bye Bugs**

Chickens are naturally happy to forage, and tasty bugs are a huge treat for them. They enjoy eating worms, beetles, crickets, larvae, slugs, spiders, and even scorpions (the small non-poisonous kinds). A mother hen will put up quite a show as she teaches her chicks about catching and eating a worm for instance, and chickens supplement their diets by scratching throughout your garden to find tasty morsels. This is great news to any avid gardener, as their activities actually loosen the soil and keep unwanted pests at bay. This will significantly cut down on your need to spray your yard with pesticides and since they poop naturally while scratching about, they even fertilize your yard for you. This brings us to the next point, fertilizer:

- **Chickens are Fertilizer Factories**

Since chickens naturally scratch all around your yard in their daily foraging activities they also naturally poop and distribute that poop. Chicken poop is naturally rich in nitrogen and makes a great additive to your compost heap. The only time that their poop needs to be managed, is when you let them roost naturally. In this case, you need to be prepared because they poop huge volumes at night while they sleep. So you may benefit from locking them in a coup at night not only to keep them safe, but also to manage where they poop, making it easier to clean up. Your neighbors might even come knocking on your door wanting some of their poop to give their lawns a dressing, since it is such an excellent fertilizer, and this again offers a potential for a small side business. If nothing else, it could partially pay for the chickens' feed.

- **Entertainment and Company**

People also keep chickens not only as a source of income or due to them being an excellent food supply, but also because chickens are entertaining to watch and can even be quite sociable. Chickens will naturally gather near you when you are chilling in the backyard, and they have loads of little antics that are entertaining to watch. Certainly, the mother hen with her brood of chicks sheltered under her wings is an endearing sight to behold. Hens have a little pecking order that they establish, and seeing them sort each other out can be quite entertaining.

Some chickens have a range of melodious sounds that they can produce, which are quite different from the loud clucking they make when they have laid an egg. They can even produce a strange almost whistling sound in their throats that is quite lovely to hear. In colder weather, they huddle together for warmth, and don't be surprised if your braver hens decide to join you in the kitchen or snuggle up next to you on the back porch. Chickens make excellent pets too.

Chickens as Pets

Chickens make for excellent pets. They love attention and enjoy being scratched. They enjoy bathing and can even swim quite well. Chickens, when properly cared for, can even live as long as eight to ten years (some even longer). Image: Daniel Tuttle on Unsplash.

Not all chickens will enjoy being hugged and held, although, when they are handled regularly from hatching age, they do come to enjoy that human contact. They will even come running when their human comes off the bus from school or gets home from work. Pet shops even sell commercially made chicken harnesses so that you can take your pet chicken for a walk. No two chickens are the same either. They do have their own personalities, and while some will be mostly content with the occasional stroke and extra morsels to eat, others will demand your attention and follow after you, seeming interested in everything that you do. Even roosters make for good pets, though you may need to keep an eye on their spurs and trim these when they get too long or dangerous.

With young children, some care should be taken when they learn about chickens. Since chickens are constant foragers, they will peck whatever is in range, including sweets, peppermints, human toes, and shiny eyes. So, with young children, you should be careful of letting them hold hens close to their faces as this might lead to accidentally being pecked in the face.

Chickens are surprisingly intelligent (if you consider that their brains are the size of a peanut)! They can learn to respond to certain words or sounds and once they have learned they can come when called, perform tricks, cuddle up, and even be an emotional support animal. Their bodies are warm and soft, making them ideal for snuggling with, and they respond well to a loving stroke (perhaps even better than a cat).

With chickens having a fast reproductive cycle, it can bring children great joy in raising chicks, without the expenses of having to spay the hens. If you decide you don't want the eggs to hatch, you can simply take them away, without the fuss and emotional drama of having to give away chicks like you would a litter of puppies. Since chickens tend to roost in the same spot every night, you can also minimize their poop being all over your house or yard, unlike dogs who need to be cleaned up after every day.

Given that chickens are soft and somewhat fragile (especially the chicks) you can encourage children to be responsible and hold their pet chickens softly. As a responsible parent, you should keep an eye on your young child to ensure that they don't harm the birds or shake them, as some children do find it funny to make the chicken's head bob. For the most part, a well-mannered child will not have any problems with being responsible for and enjoying a pet chicken.

Lastly, when deciding to keep a chicken as a pet, you may be concerned with the spread of avian influenza or bird flu. It is a real concern to keep a pet that could potentially spread a deadly disease to you or your family. In recent outbreaks of bird flu in the U.S., the blame was often placed with backyard chicken keepers as their conditions are not regulated. According to the renowned chicken author and poultry farmer, Gail Damerow (2016) bird flu is not likely to spread through backyard chicken keeping. Bird flu thrives in crowded conditions where the chickens easily spread diseases among each other. In a natural situation such as a backyard coop with a limited number of birds, or with a limited number of free-ranging birds, the chances of this deadly disease starting is limited. Still, it is good practice to keep an eye on your flock, watch for signs of disease, and take appropriate steps. Chapter six will discuss chicken health in more detail.

Chickens Pros and Cons

Okay, so you feel that you are ready to possibly start keeping chickens in your backyard, but you are not 100 percent prepared yet. Whenever making any big life decision, you should weigh up the pros and cons. Kelly from *Once a Month Meals* (2012), writes honestly about these considerations.

- **The Cons**

So the cons are not many, but they can have a hefty impact on your decision to keep chickens or not. Firstly, chickens are not born ready to produce or add economic value to your family from day one. Many chicken breeds only start laying eggs from six months old and onwards, and in the meantime, you need to still feed and care for them. Sometimes, hens can even be barren and lay no eggs. Your baby chick, that the storekeeper assured you was a hen, may turn out to be a rooster, bringing a whole new range of challenges to you.

To make healthy eggs, you need to give healthy feed to your chickens. GMO-free foods can be pricey, and depending on where you live, it may be difficult to obtain.

Setting up a shelter or coop for your feathery additions can also be a costly exercise. Chickens need space, so it can't be too small for them, or if you choose to let your chickens free-range across your yard, you may need to ensure that the fences are high enough to keep them within your premises (yes, chickens can flap enough to do short flights and scale tall walls). If you are raising chicks, you will not want to cut the hen's wings as this will limit her ability to warm her chicks in inclement weather.

Chickens can be noisy. Unlike a yapping dog that listens (sort of) when you yell at it for barking, a chicken will proudly announce to the whole world that he has found another hen, or she has laid another egg. Though cute at first, it may be less so when this happens at three A.M. in the morning. Even hens can take to crowing like a rooster, so believing that you are not going to have that problem because all your feathery babies are girls may not be entirely accurate.

As previously mentioned, chickens poop...a lot! Though this poop is really fertile and can offer benefits with fertilizing the lawn or your veggie patch, it is also smelly and your chickens will poop wherever they want, including on your windshield every night when your hens decide to roost on your car's camper rail. You will have to set aside time to clean your chickens' coop and muck out their regular spaces on a weekly basis. At times, their habit of roosting in high places can also end up being less enjoyable when your new hen decides that she will stroll into your kitchen to promptly poop on your kitchen table.

In terms of a hen's lifespan, a hen will enjoy at most two to three years of egg-laying fertility, and you will have to consider what to do with non-laying hens after that. You may feel awkward about slaughtering hens that you raised from chicks. Yet you can't have 50 chickens, so it will be up to you as the chicken keeper to make decisions about what to do with surplus hens.

- **The Pros**

Despite the ominous seeming cons, chicken keeping has several huge plus points, such as the wealth of educational knowledge that you can discover and share with your family when you start keeping chickens. If you have young children, keeping chickens in your backyard can offer a chance for your children to learn the routines and cycles of nature that we city slickers miss. Since chickens are lively and actively participate in gardening, they have more appeal to children than a "lifeless" vegetable patch. This allows children to become interested in understanding where their food comes from.

Organic eggs or organically raised chickens are more healthy and higher in nutritional value than factory-farmed poultry and eggs. Having the chickens free-range in your yard will also cut down on insects and kitchen scraps. This means that you will be limiting your carbon footprint, cut down on the distance that food needs to be transported to reach you, and helps cut down on the harmful emissions made by fertilizer factories.

Keeping chickens is also a great way to ensure that your veggies garden has sufficient fertilizer to keep your plants growing well. Now, not only will you have fresh eggs but also freshly grown vegetables right from your own garden. Keeping chickens may change the way in which you view the whole food cycle that we are all a part of. Since you will be a mini farmer, you may become more aware of the challenges that face many commercial farmers and feel a little bit more gratitude for the food on your plate. You will also begin to take immense pride in your own skills in keeping chickens and in enjoying their wealth of eggs, succulent bodies (should you keep chickens for slaughter), or you may even discover your chickens to be emotionally supportive pets, something that you had never considered them to be.

CHAPTER 2

The Art of Sustainable Living

The world has become a crowded and hungry place. The pressure is being tightened on our natural resources to help feed the masses, and our demands have far outstripped our planet's abilities to sustain us. It is no longer something that can be ignored as each of us has an impact on the sustainability of life on this planet. That may sound extreme, but it is fast becoming a reality. Just because food is commercially available does not necessarily mean that we should consume such mass-produced foods. Living sustainably means that we lessen our impact on the world's available resources by being responsible for what we eat, reusing, and creating our own food resources. This need not be a cumbersome task that will require a degree in bioengineering to accomplish.

Instead, it is something that all of us can be a part of and come to enjoy.

Sustainable Living and Why It Matters

Sustainable living means to live and use our world responsibly. Many of us neglect this responsibility and believe that we are simply a drop in a bucket, and that our personal reduction in resource use will make no difference. Yet this could not be further from the truth. Every drop counts. Every mile less that is driven to deliver food reduces pollution, and every chicken that is reared in your backyard will create a decrease in demand for eggs, fertilizers, meat, and factory farming.

According to Kassandra Smith, senior editor at Backyard Chicken Coops.com (2014), sustainable living is about "living on the Earth as lightly as possible." This is not a fad or craze that you go through in your early twenties and "get over" later in life; instead, it is a sustained way of life or a new philosophy that we all should develop. The reality is that our earth will run out of resources if we don't become responsible.

Global statistics according to the International Resource Panel indicate that many of our natural resources will be completely depleted within the next 50 to 100 years. Natural minerals such as phosphorus will be completely depleted by as early as the year 2065, meaning that there will be no more fertilizers available to facilitate the healthy growth of plants to support food production. While fresh drinking water may run out within only a few years, becoming scarce by the year 2030 (Vision Times.com, 2019).

If every person on the planet were to dramatically reduce their individual strain on our natural resources these statistics could become quite different. It is not even difficult. It just requires a mindset change and some small efforts. Raising chickens, growing a backyard vegetable garden, making your own fertilizer, collecting rainwater, and reducing your carbon emissions could all contribute to prolonging the feasibility of life on this planet.

Growing your own vegetables in your garden and raising chickens can dramatically contribute to reducing your carbon footprint. If a delivery truck carries 250 pallets of 30 egg trays each, then it transports 7,500 eggs weekly. Should your hens lay only six eggs per day, then it means that only 178 families who do likewise would result in the truck not needing to transport those eggs, saving fuel, saving on the need for packaging and minimizing pollution. Your drop in the bucket counts. Image: Nikola Jovanic on Unsplash.

We have become a society of wanting and not doing, taking and not giving back. This is where the mindset comes in. If we each take responsibility for our own impact on our environment we have a real chance to turn things around for the better. In the information age that we are living in, there really is no excuse to not live responsibly. The information on how to do so is available everywhere and with technological advances, it has become easier and even cheaper than ever to start living sustainably. Even if you don't necessarily buy into the media "hype" about the world fast approaching its expiration date due to the rapid consumption of resources, you should buy into the impact that careless living has on your wallet.

Driving fuel-guzzling cars, eating commercially produced meats and fast foods, using large quantities of gas or electricity in your home, and the rising cost of healthcare have all begun to turn the screws on our available funds for daily living. Living responsibly and sustainably will lessen this drain, although it may require an initial cash payout for some basic equipment such as a chicken coop for raising chickens, buying seeds for a vegetable garden, investing in a tank and spraying system to collect and use rainwater, and installing solar panels to collect and use solar energy. In the end, by eating healthier, you and your family will need to make less use of the healthcare system, which will also help save you money and become an investment in the quality of your lives.

Chickens and Living Sustainably

So raising chickens in your backyard not only provides you with yummy and nutritious fresh eggs, they are a real and substantial means of living sustainably, and they may be the first step towards other changes to your lifestyle and living more responsibly.

As already alluded to, chickens are a means for lowering your pressure on natural resources, since you need to buy less commercially produced chicken or eggs (if any). Chicken poop not only acts as a fertilizer, but it also restores a small quantity of phosphorus and nitrogen to the soil. According to Wikipedia (n.d.), fresh chicken manure is rich. It contains 0.8% potassium, 0.5% phosphorus, and 1.5% nitrogen. This means that processing and composting chicken manure is a valuable method to return phosphorus to the soil.

On a social side, you may be more inclined to slow down your life in order to spend more time with your chickens. This will certainly cut back on costs and pollution associated with travel on a daily basis. Many of us are quick to drive to a corner market in the morning to get eggs for breakfast, but with chickens at home, you could instead spend a quiet morning collecting fresh eggs and making a scrumptious breakfast with your family.

In social media, the catchphrase, "Reduce, reuse, and recycle," has become popular, however, few of us actively apply this philosophy to our lives. Chicken raising will make you and your family more aware of how nature follows this philosophy quite successfully. Your chickens naturally reduce their negative impact by foraging for what is available. They scratch happily in the dirt for bugs, worms, and weevils. A bucket of scraps from the kitchen is a feast to them, and they come running to recycle this into usable products such as juicy flesh, fresh eggs, and fertile manure. Your chickens will happily drink rainwater (though it's up to you to check that it's fresh), and they will make use of whatever is available to construct their nests in. In setting up your chicken-keeping environment and routine, you should start by following their example. It may not be necessary to buy everything to set up a commercial styled chicken friendly backyard. Rather you could reuse existing resources.

Even an old and rusted car could be converted into a fertile garden or chicken coop, becoming kitch, practical, and sustainable. By adding some mesh wire to the windows, removing some panels and lining the floor, you could create a functional and safe home for your chickens while stopping an old car from wasting away on a landfill. Image: Diane Helentjaris on Unsplash.

Buying commercially produced chicken products, eggs, and vegetables comes with the added burden of these products coming in plastic, polystyrene, and foil packages that add to the global pandemic of waste production. These byproducts associated with buying your food commercially are not only harmful to our planet, but also drain other natural resources such as fossil fuels required to make these products and the cost of transporting the packages to the food processing plants. By raising chickens and possibly growing some of your own food, you remove a very harmful link in the commercial machine. In including your children in this process of responsible living, you will ensure that future generations are committed and informed about the need for sustainable living. When we are born into something we are more likely to perpetuate it. We were born into the generation of "use and want" things. Perhaps with every chick that your child rears, and with every egg that they collect in the morning, they may be re-born into a generation that does not use, but rather recycles and rebuilds the world that we have destroyed through our ignorance and lack of responsibility.

CHAPTER 3

What to Expect When You're Eggspecting

Okay, so you are ready to start raising chickens. Your backyard has been swept clean, and you can't wait for the first feathery hens to arrive...but are you ready? There are still a few matters to consider before taking the poultry plunge. You need to be fully informed about what the law says on keeping chickens, what your responsibilities will be, how to negate the cons of keeping chickens and make sure that your backyard will be chicken heaven, not a death sentence for your flock.

Readying Your Space for Chickens

Chickens will need so much more than just their coop. Though the coop may be the most substantial cash layout, you need to consider the whole of your backyard and ensure that it is chicken friendly and safe. You may need to walk your grounds and create a list of things to do, plants to move or remove, possible crawl spaces where the chickens could get stuck or escape your yard, and list plants you need to cultivate such as long grass. Here is a checklist of some potential issues to consider in your backyard:

- **Security**

Are your chickens going to be safe? Will they have shelter from inclement weather, and potential predators? Can you ensure that they will not leave the backyard? Do you need to clip their wings, or enclose the space with wire mesh or shade cloth?

Cats, dogs, crows, falcons, rats, coyotes, and many other pillagers can threaten the safety of your flock. Ensure that your chickens will be safe, especially at night. Image: Clement Falize on Unsplash.

- **Safety From Poisoning**

Chickens are omnivores, which means that they will eat almost anything. Young chickens and chicks are especially foolish and will happily peck at just about anything they find on the ground. You need to ensure that your backyard is free from harmful substances such as rat poison, cigarette butts, kitchen scraps that are poisonous to them, and plants that may be toxic to chickens. Some of the ornamental plants in your backyard may pose a risk to your chickens should they eat them accidentally. Usually, adult chickens will quickly avoid something that doesn't "taste" right to them. However, if they are not on a balanced diet, or are food-deprived, they may eat what is available and suffer the consequences. Plants such as azaleas, daffodils, foxgloves, honeysuckle, ivy, and jasmine can be quite toxic to chickens. You would be wise to move these plants from your backyard, or effectively close them off. Take care with your compost heap, as you may be adding kitchen scraps to it that are highly toxic to chickens. Rather keep the compost heap in a container that you can close up, or keep it fenced off from the chickens.

- **Create a Yard for Your Chickens**

Your flock will require certain elements in your yard. They will not thrive on a neatly paved backyard, and in that case, you will need to think long and hard about how you will make your yard friendly for chickens. Chickens need vegetation in three layers to meet their needs. Firstly, they will need a canopy of trees to shelter in, roost in, and play around in. Low hanging trees are ideal with branches that will encourage your chickens to fly up and enjoy. Secondly, they will need a variety of shrubs to hide under, peck at, and explore. Choosing shrubs that are chicken friendly will be a huge benefit as chickens love to peck at everything. Thirdly, your chickens will need a ground covering that is beneficial to scratching, sand bathing, and simply resting on. A well-grown lawn or grassy patches of pet-friendly grass is ideal as your chickens will appreciate the tasty leaves and seeds when these appear. Chickens will also love exploring your vegetable patch, so you may need to keep this in mind as they will peck at anything from carrots, salad, and strawberries, to whatever happens to be flowering. You should also take care in choosing your veggies to plant as some vegetables are not beneficial to the health of your chickens, such as onions, though this will be further discussed in chapter six.

- **Consider Your Existing Animals**

If you are considering keeping chickens, the chances are that they will not be your only family pets. Your family may already have a dog, cat, pet snake, or even other exotic pets. You will need to keep in mind that your existing pets could threaten your chickens. Dogs and cats remain wild animals with a killer instinct, and should the opportunity to hunt present itself, chances are that dear old rover might destroy your prized hens as soon as the backdoor opens. This is an eventuality that you need to be prepared for. You may need to find an effective way to isolate your predatory pets from your chickens such as fencing off the backyard completely, and making sure to manage your animals to minimize danger and conflict. It must be pointed out that many kittens and puppies are quite happy to socialize with chickens and chicks, though human supervision is advised to limit the potential for drama.

In addition to your own pets, you need to be informed of the local animals and wildlife in your neighborhood. Hawks are predators to consider as they love juicy feathered morsels such as chicks scratching in the dirt. Closing off the backyard with some form of wire mesh or PVC webbing will save you from losing your flock to aerial predators. Image: Thijs Schouten on Unsplash.

- **Geological Location**

If you live in the far northern reaches of Canada, you may want to reconsider keeping chickens. It is unlikely that they will survive harsh winter temperatures, while in countries with extreme heat, you may need to provide special care to keep your chickens from dying of heat exposure. Should you live in a location with strong rainfall, you need to ensure that your chickens are safe from flooding, and ensure that the chickens and chicks are kept warm and dry. This could all add up to a substantial amount of time and possibly a lot of cash to buy heating lamps and warming cages, which you may not be ready for. However, it must be said that chickens are quite resourceful birds, and they quickly get into a routine such as marching to their lockable coop at night to be safely locked up. Thankfully, mother hens are insanely protective over their chicks, which also helps negate some minor predators and climate factors such as the occasional thunderstorm that drenches your chicks.

What the Law Says About Chicken Raising

Needless to say, raising chickens can lead to a legal nightmare if you do not first investigate the laws, bylaws and city ordinances that apply to your area of residence. Most local laws allow for the keeping of hens and chicks, but either forbid roosters or limit them to one rooster per coop. It makes sense as not everyone wants an entire neighborhood's twenty roosters crowing at the crack of dawn on a Sunday morning. Hens do cackle, especially when they have laid an egg, but they usually don't crow as incessantly as most roosters do. Happily, you don't need roosters to get eggs.

Your local laws may limit how many chickens you may keep according to the square footage of your yard. Again, it makes sense as this will prevent people from getting overzealous and keeping a hundred hens in a ten square foot yard. This would lead to the creation of disease rife environments and lead to noise pollution as well as unsanitary conditions, not to mention animal abuse.

Local laws usually stipulate what to do with birds that die, and may require that your property be inspected by health inspectors on a regular basis. This is not only for the health of the community, but also for you and your family's health. To ensure compliance to regulations, you may be required to pay a license fee, just as some cities and counties require that you pay for a dog license.

There may also be stipulations about what your coop may look like, and it may even need to pass a building inspector's report. You may also have to ensure that your coop is a certain distance from your neighbor's property, while in some areas you may have to confine your hens to the coop and no free-ranging is allowed.

Selling eggs can also be subject to your local laws, and you should check these carefully at your local municipal or government offices. Most areas will prohibit the slaughter of chickens, so if you plan on raising chickens for meat, you will have to find out what your local laws say, or make an arrangement with a local slaughterhouse to slaughter and defeather your birds for you once they are large enough. More than likely, there will be some regulations on the noise levels that your hens may engage in, and just like your teenagers could get into trouble for being too rowdy, your hens can also bring the police knocking.

Depending on where you live, there could be some health-related regulations regarding the storage of chicken feed, chicken manure, and the size of the coop per the number of chickens. You may even have to ensure that there is fire equipment available in case the coop catches on fire as it will likely have straw bedding in for the hens. Most of the laws are based on ensuring a safe and harmonious society, not on being punitive or overly restrictive. However, laws do become outdated and might be based on a few politicians' own personal aversions of poultry in city limits, in which case, you will need to take legal steps to get your dream of having your own backyard chickens.

In extreme cases, you may need to consult with a lawyer specializing in property zoning to get the right to keep chickens. There are also many activist groups that can help you appeal if the laws in your area are unfavorable to keeping chickens in your backyard. However, it is best to find out all the details before you take the plunge and purchase your first chickens. It would be a terrible loss to invest your time, money, and effort into setting up your backyard chickens only to be told that they are illegal and will be confiscated. You could even end up with a fine.

Other Considerations and Dealing With the Down Sides of Keeping Chickens

Keeping chickens in the confines of your backyard certainly has many benefits, however, as previously pointed out, there are some cons too. They can become a nuisance if left to breed unchecked, should you have both hens and a rooster. As with any animal or pet, they can become loud and lead to your neighbors complaining. If you do not have a plan in place for cleaning up their coop, they will also become smelly and attract flies and rodents. If you do not feed them sufficient quantities of diverse and nutritious pellets and kitchen scraps, they will demolish your garden. It can prove expensive to keep them if you don't plan ahead and keep an eye on your backyard chicken mini-farm. And, lastly, if you don't provide a safe environment for your chickens, you may end up facing a traumatic financial loss should a predator invade your backyard and slaughter all your beloved hens.

There are, however, effective ways to minimize the downsides of keeping chickens. Effective planning is one way to deal with potential problems. Here's how you could minimize each of the above cons or turn them into a pro instead:

- **Excessive Breeding**

Most urban areas have laws that prohibit the keeping of roosters exactly to stop backyard breeding. You don't need roosters to lay eggs. In fact, most commercial eggs are unfertilized anyway. As a kid you may even have tried to hatch a store-bought egg, to have a chick to keep as a pet, to no avail. If you do keep a rooster, then there are some alternatives to ending up with a whole clutch of chicks marching along your driveway. You can mark the eggs as they are being laid and remove some to use in your cooking. It is perfectly okay to eat a fertilized egg, as long as you remove it from the nest on the day that it is laid to prevent it from being a half-brooded egg.

You could also trade older chicks with other breeders to introduce genetic variation into your flock, or regularly send birds to slaughter and enjoy succulent meats from the butcher. There is also a market for selling pullets or female chicks to other people who want to start keeping chickens. Even some pet stores will happily take on a clutch of older chicks to resell for you. There is no reason to be stuck with more chickens than you can't keep. It's advisable to keep no more than four to six hens in an average-sized backyard, and the laws in most areas indicate this as the limit. Kindly refrain from keeping only one chicken as chickens are social creatures, and your single chicken will be lonely and could end up being quite stressed, fall sick, and die.

- **Noise Problems**

Chickens, like most birds, do tend to be a bit noisy. As a responsible chicken owner, you can ensure that your chicken coop is well insulated with thickened plank walls. You can also surround it with shrubs, and keep it as far away from the neighbors as possible. It is also wise to keep your chickens penned up at night and only release them later in the morning–preferably once your neighbors have left for work. There are automated chicken doors available that work on a timer, allowing you to release your flock even when you are at work yourself. If nothing else, you can certainly sweeten things with the neighbors by sending them some fresh eggs or meat every once in a while.

- **Cleanliness**

If you regularly clean the chicken coop and neaten up your backyard, you will not have a problem with keeping chickens and avoiding any unpleasant odors. According to Quora.com an average chicken will "produce" 1/3lb per day of poop. When you multiply that by the number of chickens that you keep, it becomes obvious that cleaning up after your chickens should be a daily task. You need to keep the manure in a covered area to cut down on any unpleasant smells and for hygiene reasons. Once you have a sizable amount of manure gathered you should decide on what to do with it. Likely, your chickens will produce more than you can effectively use in your own yard or veggie garden. You could consider selling bags of well-ripened chicken manure to other gardeners, and some garden services will happily either buy or fetch manure from you on a regular basis.

Should your hens be breeding, you will need to clean more regularly, especially if your chickens are bound to the coop. It would also be wise to use a product such as Sanisec to sanitize the coop area and prevent the spread of diseases that might lead to your flock becoming sick. As a bonus, these sanitizing products also have fly repellent properties. It is advised to look for something that is made from natural ingredients to prevent an allergic reaction in your chickens. This would help greatly with maintaining the area where you keep chickens neat and tidy, ready for unexpected property inspections.

- **Saving Your Garden**

Chickens are curious creatures, and since they lack hands, they tend to peck at everything that interests them. It may not always be because they are hungry, although hunger can drive them to do so in excess. As a chicken keeper, you may need to accept that some plants are too tempting to chickens, and you may need to protect these plants at times by covering them up. If you keep flowering plants like ornamental sunflowers, oregano, and strawberries, you may need to ensure that the chickens don't have access to them. Chickens will supplement their diet with a wide array of interesting and nutritious plants naturally. Remember, a chicken is not being naughty when it pecks at your plants, it's simply doing what nature has programmed it to do. You can minimize the damage by ensuring that your chickens have an interesting environment to perch on, play on, and providing them with sufficiently diverse foods to eat.

- **Cutting Costs**

Finding organically grown and processed chicken feed may be an expensive cost, and you would be wise to supplement their diet along the way with suitable kitchen scraps. Selling eggs and manure is just one way to have your chickens pay for themselves though. Using effective chicken feeders and positioning their feed out of the sun and rain will also cut down on wastage. If you buy in bulk and store the feed in a sealed container, you will also save some money. Clubbing in with another backyard chicken keeper in your area to buy large scale quantities could also be an option to consider.

One of the largest threats and costs is when your chickens get sick, die, or are slaughtered by predators. Apart from the obvious vet bills of a sick or injured chicken, you may also need to replace a hen with another younger chicken. This would mean that you may not enjoy the benefits of having eggs every day as the new hen may still need time to mature and reach laying age. Chickens also have a limited time that they can lay eggs in, and you may end up with hens that can no longer produce eggs but still cost you money to feed. You will need to decide what to do in that case as you may need to replace them to still keep having eggs but might not be able to afford to keep so many chickens. Well socialized mature hens can be rehomed as pets, if you are not inclined towards slaughtering your own birds.

- **Keeping Predators Away**

To ensure the safety of your feathered flock, you need to inspect their area every day for new gaps in the fencing, or signs that predators are becoming interested in them. Your neighbor's dog might be tunneling into your backyard for a snack, and to avoid conflict, you need to be alert to this. It's better to take precautions than face a huge loss or traumatic incident. While there may be no predators in your area when you start with chickens, you might be surprised when a family of owls takes up residence in a nearby tree, with their eyes fixed on your young chicks. It is a good idea to remain alert and ask your neighbors to help you keep an eye open for trouble that may be brewing. Even young children in the neighborhood may prove a problem if they are not accustomed to chickens or respecting your property boundaries. Your own pets could even mistakenly believe that a movable feast is residing in their backyard. It would be naive to expect Fluffy to immediately get along with your new chickens, thus, it is best to ensure that they are kept apart.

Keeping chickens is a rewarding and stimulating hobby for many. However, the uninitiated should become informed and educated about matters such as the law, costs, dangers, and challenges to ensure that they have a realistic expectation going forward to purchasing their first chicken. Once you are fully informed, financially and emotionally prepared, and have gotten all the role players on board, namely your neighbors, family, and local government officials, you are ready to start planning for making a home for your chickens.

CHAPTER 4

The Coop

It is said that home is where the heart is, and if your chickens love their home, they will love to stay there. One of the biggest fears of chicken owners is a stray chicken that could be stolen, eaten by predators, run over by vehicles, and having an angry neighbor call because your chicken drowned in their swimming pool. To prevent disaster and create backyard bliss, you will need to decide on an appropriate home or coop for your chickens.

Choosing a Coop Design

Whether you end up buying a prefabricated chicken coop or building your own, you need to consider the requirements of your chickens. Will your chickens require more shelter from the heat, or from rain? Do you need to have the coop open automatically for letting them in or out, and should your coop include a feeding area for when you are not able to let them out? Should you coop be mobile to enable better cleaning or to move the coop seasonally? These are just a few of the questions that you will need to consider when selecting a coop design.

If you have basic woodworking skills, or are quite handy, you will be able to build a suitable coop at a fraction of the cost of a commercially available coop. However, if you have limited time available or were born with two left thumbs, you may find it much more convenient to order a coop online that requires minimal assembly. What should be kept in mind is that some municipalities will require that you submit a building plan for your chicken coop or chicken run. This is to ensure that the construction isn't dangerous or harmful to the environment.

There are many coop designs on the Internet, some with free downloadable plans that you can easily submit to your local government offices for approval, should this be required. However, you should consider the following before choosing a design:

- **Size**

On average, and according to some laws, you should have three to four square feet of floor space per chicken in your coop. If they are permanently being cooped, perhaps due to your local laws or ordinances not permitting free-range chickens, you will have to at least double the space per chicken. Should you choose a larger breed chicken, you will need to increase this space further still.

If you plan on starting with two or three chickens and plan on expanding with chicks later, you may need to consider a coop construction that allows for you to add units later as your flock grows.

Finally, when deciding on the size and shape of your coop, keep in mind that you will need to clean the coop. If you build it as a hobbit-sized coop, you will struggle to clean it since you will need to crawl into tight spaces. Instead, create a coop that you can easily reach into, or plan side panels that are on hinges that you can open to clean up those hard to reach spots.

- **Placement**

Before you buy or start building a coop, you should consider where in your backyard you would place this coop. Will it be in a permanently sunny spot or under trees? Do you experience strong winds in your area, and will you be visiting the coop often during the day? It may be a good idea to keep watch on your intended location for the coop over a week or more, so that you can observe how the local weather is in that area. If it is located under the roof's downpipes, you may end up with a flooded coop, and if it should receive full sun all day long, it may become stuffy and create an environment prone to sickness and heat-stressed chickens. Although coops can be made to be mobile, you should make the intended location a top consideration, as moving a fully assembled coop can be a difficult, if not impossible exercise. Keep in mind that some local laws insist on coops being free-standing or mobile.

- **Must-Haves and Nice-to-Haves**

Now that you are planning your coop, you should consider the things that it simply must have, and also list the things that you might not have funds for at the moment, but you would like to add in the future.

Must-haves include a suitable nesting box per hen (although they do share), ventilation access points, shelter, and a feeder or watering spot. Hens tend to naturally choose a nesting area above the ground, and initially, you could even appropriate an old shoebox or tomato crate for a nesting box. Just make sure that the nesting box is sturdy and line it with suitable nesting material such as hay. With the feeder and waterer, ensure that the feeder allows for natural scratching impulses and is low on the ground, while ensuring that the water feeder is sturdy and won't get knocked down during the day–leaving your chickens waterless.

Nice to haves might extend to having a covered perching area for when the weather is poor, opening the coop out onto a chicken run that would keep your chickens safe, a level area, preferably in the sun, where your chickens can have a dust bath, installing boards under the perches to catch poop and help with cleaning, and perhaps also lights in case you need to check on the chickens at night. If you live in a colder climate, you may also want to add warming or red lights to help keep the eggs warm and increase the number of eggs that hatch.

- **Budget**

Lastly, you should consider the available cash that you can put into buying or building a chicken coop. If you have some cash now, and expect that you may have more later, then building a coop that can be expanded upon is ideal. If you are cash strapped, you may need to see what waste materials you can scrounge up to build your own coop. Materials that you could get as waste or trash from different businesses include tomato crates, construction pallets, left-over mesh wire, and shipping containers. Even second-hand tires can be added to make a perch or nesting boxes for smaller hens. Old furniture pieces can be converted to make coops with doors removed to allow ventilation. Even an old dog kennel can become a suitable coop for two or three hens that can free-range during the day. Shopping around at garage sales or thrift stores might help you find ways to cut corners in your coop design. Always remember though that your local laws might impose certain restrictions, so keep the safety and health of your chickens in mind.

Even an old hot-house or unused arbor may be converted into a very luxurious coop. It doesn't have to cost a fortune and as long as your chickens will be happy and

legal, you should do what works for them. Image: Sophie Mikat on Unsplash.

Cooped Up Vs Free Range

Free-range chickens are probably happier than being cooped up, hence the expression. However, your circumstances and local laws may prevent this from being a possibility in your area. In that case, you will have to ensure that your chicken coop is suitable for long term habitation by your chickens. You can certainly add exercise and fun to your chickens' lives by including a chicken run that adjoins to their coop.

If your chickens are free-range, they are more likely to fall prey to predators such as hawks, crows, cats, coyotes, and dogs. You will have to take steps to ensure that they are protected, or only let them free-range when you are nearby to keep an eye. For those keeping chickens as pets, there are even commercial harnesses available so that you can take your pet chicken for walks to the park.

Chickens tend to stay near their regular feeding areas, but they do fly and will likely perch on the perimeter fence around your property. If your neighbors are happy with this, you are very fortunate. Mostly, you will need to ensure that your chickens stay in your yard. This might mean clipping their wings, or installing wire tops to your fences that prevent the chickens from landing comfortably. Chickens have large feet, as birds go, and they need a large or thickened object to perch on. A thin wire top or sturdy mesh attached to your fences will dissuade your chickens from flapping up.

Keeping your chickens within a specified area can be done by installing PVC pipes with plastic or construction mesh to keep them contained. It will also keep most small dogs from venturing too close to your chickens.

Creating a Chicken Run

A chicken run is exactly as the name says, a place where your chickens can run and move about. Chickens also need exercise to keep them healthy. If they are kept in confinement it is mentally and physically detrimental to their health. Most modern coop designs are based on a raised chicken coop with the area beneath it being used as a chicken run. Others extend outward into an adjacent chicken run. Though not as good as free-ranging, it will allow your chickens the opportunity to move, and socialize.

If you have the budget you can make a chicken run as large as or even part of your house. You can include all sorts of fun places to perch, and even include water features and rolling spots. Since you can control where your chickens will perch and mostly poop, you can include poop boards that will make cleaning the coop and run a cinch. Chicken runs are usually closed at the top to keep predators out, but you need to keep the entrances well secured to keep nosy dogs, cats, and coyotes out. As a handy tip, you may decide that on days when the weather is nice, and you are faffing around your garden, you want to let your chickens out to explore for a while. It's a good idea to have some industrial-grade plastic mesh available that you can use to cordon off a safe zone in your garden for them. This could be a practical way to give them a temporary free-range experience, while still keeping them safe.

Roosting and Brooding

Chickens naturally like to perch, and it can be great fun to watch the young chicks learn to fly up to sit on whatever is available, even their mother's back. It almost becomes a kind of dominance game between chicks to see who can balance on a new object the longest. Certainly, it may be a natural instinct to sit high to watch for the approach of potential predators. Image: Arisa Chattasa on Unsplash.

A favored perch is where your chickens will tend to spend the most time, and it is also where they will poop the most. To ensure that you have happy and healthy chickens, you should provide them with suitable perching places. In selecting things to let them perch on, keep in mind that these need to be suited to the shape of a chicken's feet, as they struggle to perch on narrow things, although they will certainly try. Old broomsticks, wooden planks, thick rope spanning a gap and lovely branches are all excellent examples of perching places that will bring pleasure to your chickens. They should also be built at different heights, especially if you arc going to be keeping chicks who can't flap as high as the adult chickens yet. Perching allows your chickens to feel safe.

Brooding is a term that is used to describe a hen that is preparing to lay eggs, or is already nesting on a clutch of eggs. They tend to get really plump and clucky when this happens. To ensure that your hen can happily begin laying eggs, you should provide her with a suitable place to make her nest. It should be warm, slightly dark, and out of the way. A coup is an ideal place to build nesting boxes, but you can also place some old baskets lined with soft hay for her to inspect. She will thank you for your consideration of her brooding by giving you fresh eggs and healthy chicks.

Cleaning

This is probably the chore associated with chicken keeping that is the least anticipated, and people new to keeping chickens will be shocked at the sheer volume of manure that a few hens can produce in a week. This becomes even more apparent when those hens are confined to a coop or a chicken run. It is best practice to clean your chicken coop on a regular basis, preferably sooner than once a week. At this point, it may be very handy to have a smaller cage where you can confine your chickens until you have finished with the task. If you have hens brooding on some eggs, you may need to clean around them carefully without disturbing them too much, or you will face one hell of a ruckus as the disturbed hen protests at your inconsiderate behavior.

For basic cleaning you will need the following tools:

- ❏ A spade

- ❏ A rough bristled broom

- ❏ Heavy-duty plastic gloves

- ❏ A bucket to scoop the manure into

- ❏ Canvas bags to store the manure in for selling or disposal

- ❏ A bag of river sand

- ❏ A mild detergent to wash the worst places

- ❏ A garden hose to wash areas that need extensive cleaning

- ❏ A supply of sanitizing powder such as Sanisec

The basic approach would be to scrape the excess manure off the poop boards that you have installed under the perching areas. Following this, you would check for any other areas where there are large mounds of poop that needs collecting. Deposit the manure in the canvas bags. If necessary use the detergent and garden hose to clean any particularly soiled areas. Make sure to properly hose away any soapy residue. Lightly dust the area with the sanitizing powder. This will ensure that you can clean with ease next time, and also eliminate some of the smell from the coop. As an added bonus, it will also ensure your chickens stay healthy, and help deter insects like mites. If necessary, add a fresh coating of river sand in the rolling areas and under the perches as this will help keep everything tidy and make your next cleaning so much easier.

When cleaning your coop it is advisable to wear gloves at all times as chicken manure can contain traces of salmonella and campylobacter, which can cause bacterial infections. For this reason, always wash your hands after cleaning the coop and handling your chickens–even when you have been wearing gloves. If you have dogs that mix with the chickens, it is also advised that you discourage them from licking or eating the chicken droppings.

Keeping a coop tidy and sanitary is a major responsibility when raising chickens at home. It can offer a range of useful family activities, which could include catching the chickens to contain them in the smaller cage before cleaning, seeing who can collect the most manure, and examining all the beautiful feathers that you will find in the coop to name but a few. When there are smaller chicks about, it can be a whole load of fun to scoop up the fluffy bundles for safekeeping with their mum until their home has been cleaned again. If you approach the chore of cleaning the coop with a fun and entertaining spirit, it will not become an arduous task, and you will have a better chance of involving the whole family. If everyone benefits from the chickens through eggs, juicy meat, or entertaining companionship, then everyone should be involved in cleaning the coop–it isn't a punishment.

If you decide to keep free-range chickens there will still be some clean-up involved. Remember, chickens will still find places to perch on. Rather provide them readily available perches such as poles, low shrubs, and small crates. If you don't, you may not like where your chickens choose to perch and poop. There is nothing as unsightly or smelly as a yard where there is chicken poop running down the walls of your house as your chickens have decided to roost in the rafters. If you install interesting perching places for your chickens, you will also be able to place some strategic poop boards that can be easily cleaned. In a free-range environment, your chickens will naturally perch close to the area where they are fed regularly–so use this to your advantage.

With sufficient planning before you begin keeping chickens, there will be fewer unpleasant surprises for you. It may require a mind shift, and the first time that you clean the coop you may begin to doubt the wisdom of your choice to raise chickens. However, when weighing up those 10 or 20 minutes that it takes to clean up the coop against daily entertainment, a healthy and nutritious food supply, and an activity that can bring real quality time back to your family–there should be no doubt in your mind that you did the right thing.

CHAPTER 5

Choosing Your Chickens

Choosing a type and breed of chicken may be more complicated than you initially imagine. Chickens come in a wide variety of sizes, colors, and temperaments. What may look pretty may not be best suited to your lifestyle and needs. You will need to consider what type of chicken you can afford, their suitability to your type of coop and local climate, and their appropriateness to your needs. Whether you require eggs, or want to raise some chickens for slaughter, you need to find the breed that is best for your needs.

Types and Breeds of Chickens

From the Ameraucana, Andalusian, Araucana, and Australorp, there are a wide variety of chickens available from respectable chicken dealers, agricultural suppliers, and pet shops in the U.S. Each have their own temperament and unique pros and cons. Before choosing your chicken breed to invest in, you need to consider the following:

❏ What do you require from the chicken? Eggs? Meat? Companionship?

❏ What environment can you offer the chicken? Small or large spaces? Adverse climates with heavy rain or snow?

❏ What hazards do you have that your chicken will have to deal with? Do they need to socialize well with your other animals? Will there be young children around that may occasionally chase after the chickens?

Respectable sources recommend that beginners look at a breed such as the Araucana or Australorp for domestic raising. Both breeds are friendly and curious by nature. The Araucana lays a distinct blue to green colored egg, and it has a hardy enough temperament to make them well-suited to have if you have pets or small children. They do not scare as easily, which will cut down on the noise levels somewhat (The Happy Chicken Coop.com, 2019). When a chicken is scared, the whole world tends to know it. The Araucana also does well in the feeding department and forages quite successfully, meaning that you will be able to spend less money on feeding, thus making them a cost-effective breed. They lay around 200 medium-sized eggs per year, which is ample for an average family's use. As a bonus, they are also cold-resistant, making them suitable to the northern climates where snow is a given.

If you are looking for high egg production, the Australorp is a very good choice. It is the current world record layer, with an astounding 364 eggs per year by one hen! They also offer a decent sized bird for slaughter, however, you must keep in mind that birds raised for slaughter require much more feeding.

The Ameraucana is a crossing bred from the Araucana but is slightly more hardy with more fertile eggs. They are curious and easily become pets, however, they do not respond well to surprises or fast-moving children. Hence, you may have to look at another breed if you have kids or other pets. On the egg side, they lay around 150 blue colored eggs a year.

If you are looking for something a little more ornamental to free-range in your yard and socialize with your family while also producing a steady supply of eggs, then the double-laced Barnevelder is a breed to consider. They have beautiful feathers and are highly social birds. They are especially fond of children and make great snugglers. They don't lay eggs as prolifically as the other breeds but will produce an egg every second to third day. You may need to keep a mixed flock if you want a better egg yield.

Black Copper Marans are also worth investigating due to their highly social and docile nature that combines with great egg laying potential. They are more active, and they would suit a large yard with other pets. Since they forage well they are also quite a low cost to keep. They average around 200 eggs per year, making them well suited to those who plan on selling some eggs.

If you are faced with a slightly more challenging set up regarding your yard space and proximity to the neighbors, you may consider the Black Star hybrid chickens. These are specifically bred from other successful chicken breeds, and the male and female chicks are each a distinct color. This is good news if you need to ensure that you don't end up with a rooster. They also gift their owners with a prolific egg-laying potential of 300 large to extra-large eggs per year! As an added bonus, they are quiet by nature and usually only put up a slight fuss when they are announcing the arrival of a new egg in the morning.

Should you only desire to keep chickens for meat and eggs with limited social interaction, but you want pluck for your buck, then the Brown Leghorn is your go-to bird. These large-sized chickens are not particularly friendly and can be hard to catch, however, they have an excellent conversion of feed into flesh and can be slaughtered at 16 weeks. They also lay numerous eggs, tallying in at 280 eggs a year. On the downside, since they are flighty, they will be a bit noisier, and you will need a larger yard or very tolerant neighbors to keep them.

The last breed that is worth a mention is the Buckeye chicken. It is an all-rounder, delivering 200 eggs a year, and a good-sized bird will measure in at seven to nine pounds for slaughter. They make great pets, and they are also exceptionally well adjusted to the cold. They will lay eggs all year round.

There are certainly many more breeds available in the U.S., and many are decent egg layers, while others are succulent meat producers. When deciding on the breed that you think is best suited, you should also consider their feed consumption, foraging abilities, temperament, hardiness, and noise production (flighty birds tend to be noisy birds).

Choosing the Best Chicken for You

Chickens can be surprisingly intimidating to someone who is not familiar with their mannerisms and personalities. When choosing a chicken, as a beginner, you should choose something that is easy to work with, has a docile nature, and will become quite tame to help with the catching and treating your chickens. Image: Desiree Fawn on Unsplash.

When choosing a chicken breed the worst decision you can make is to buy something that you don't even know the breed of. Well-meaning individuals may even bless you with chicks, but this can be a curse in disguise. Breeds of chickens have definite differences in temperament and value. If you are serious about enjoying the financial and health gains of keeping your own chickens, you need to be equally serious about picking a suitable breed of chicken.

Some chicken breeds can be dangerous to keep around young children, and you should avoid this at all costs. Breeds like the Game bird varieties are bred for the exclusive goal of producing large and ferocious roosters that can protect their hens from predators. If you are not knowledgeable about raising such chickens it is best to steer clear. A fully matured rooster, depending on the breed, can have spurs the size of kitchen knives, and they can easily cut into the unwitting human who tries to handle them. Sadly, this also means that cockfighting is still a hugely successful, though cruel and illegal, blood sport.

Thanks to the Internet, you can easily research the different chicken breeds to find information on the temperament and care for each. Thus, there is no excuse to make an uninformed decision.

How Many Chickens and Where to Get Them

When deciding on the size of your intended flock, you should consider these questions to help guide you to an informed decision.

1. What will their purpose be? Eggs, meat, and/or companionship?

2. How large is the area available to keep them in?

3. How much attention can you give them?

4. How often will you require eggs?

5. How often do you plan to slaughter a bird?

6. What do the laws applicable to your area say?

7. What can you afford in terms of feeding?

8. Is there enough supplementation to feeding available in terms of kitchen scraps and free-range foraging?

9. Do you have challenges that your chickens will have to deal with such as inclement weather, pets, and children?

10. How much time do you have to clean the coop, run, and free-range areas per week?

Though you will doubtlessly have many more questions that arise as you start chicken shopping, these are the most essential to answer before actually buying your flock of birds. When answering these questions it may be useful to consider the choices between meat producers and egg layers separately.

- **Egg Layers**

If you should require one egg per day per person, you can factor in how many hens to keep to maintain a steady supply. Baring in mind that chickens do not lay non-stop, you need to keep a flock of varying ages to ensure egg production does not drop off as your hen ages. Should you have a large family, regular visitors, bake often, or want eggs to sell, you need to find a suitable breed such as the Australorp that produces a constant supply of eggs. For an average family of four people, keeping four to five Australorp hens should provide an ample supply of eggs for their own use. There will be transition periods when a hen might stop laying, or a hen might be too old, in which case, you need to introduce a younger hen to the yard to ensure future production.

Egg-laying hens require slightly less space than your larger breeds that are bred for meat production. Your coop set up will also require more laying boxes and regular feeding to encourage egg-laying. If you are serious about getting large, nutritious, and regular eggs, you will need to feed a special brooding mix to supplement your hens sufficiently.

If you are expanding your chicken keeping, you may desire to hatch the eggs and have chicks to grow your flock with. You will need to keep one rooster, if the law permits that in your area, or buy fertilized eggs that your hens can hatch. Once your chicks arrive, you will need to be a bit more hands-on to ensure that the chicks survive and feed appropriate size crushed chicken feeds that the chicks can safely eat. You may also need to be more careful about what scraps to feed from the kitchen for a few weeks. This could cost you more money in terms of buying feeds.

If you decide on a chicken breed for laying and hatching eggs, and assuming that you are permitted to keep a rooster, you may need to install warming lights in the coop to ensure that the eggs can weather inclement days when there is rain. Again, this can be a financial lay-out that you should consider. Even adult chickens can die off if the weather turns foul, so you need to keep your local climate in mind and choose a breed suited to that.

- **Meat Producers**

Should you want a bird that grows fast and offers succulent meat, you will have some different considerations when determining how many to keep. If you are buying young chicks from a supplier and rearing them to slaughter every 16 weeks, you will need to be aware that this will be costly in terms of feeds. These birds require more space, so you will be limited not in terms of how much meat you need, but rather by how many chickens you can legally keep per square footage of your coop. The rule of thumb is three square feet per chicken in a chicken coop. Free-range chickens require more space, averaging in at 10 square feet per chicken. A coop can allow you to keep more chickens since you can create a double or triple story coop, however, the laws of your area might restrict this according to the building codes.

If you decide to raise chicks for slaughter, you need to have an effective management and feeding regime in place. Chicks have a high mortality rate, with the age of eight to 20 weeks being the worst time resulting in a 20 percent mortality rate. This can be from unsafe conditions, disease, predation, inappropriate feeding, and poor weather conditions. Younger chicks are especially susceptible to cold weather. This will all need to be considered when you plan on letting your hens brood their eggs for hatching.

- **Care and Maintenance**

A serious consideration for raising chickens, whether for eggs or meat, is the task of cleaning and maintaining their areas. If you only have ten minutes a day to feed and clean your chicken coop, it would be advisable to stick to a small flock of docile birds that you can easily close up and empty out the poop boards before heading to work in the morning. It would be best to stick to around four hens for laying in this case. Struggling with small chicks would be ill-advised. If you still want to slaughter the occasional bird, then you may want to consider a dual-purpose breed, where you can slaughter a hen once she has aged beyond a viable egg production age.

Thanks to the Internet, you can order most chicken breeds online from breeding farms, mass producers, and even smaller co-ops. You can order chickens aged from fertilized eggs, day-old chicks, and slightly older pullets to fully grown chickens. Should you want a chicken to keep as a pet, you can find many up for adoption from humane societies and other charities.

In choosing carefully and with full information considered regarding your choice of chicken, you can eliminate many problems before they start. Poorly chosen chickens can cost you a fortune in unexpected expenses relating to their care, health, and feeding. In making a choice regarding the breed of chicken, it may also be a great idea to go have a chat with your local vet to find out what they recommend, and whether there are any chicken born diseases prevalent in your area. Certainly, your health and the health of your chickens should be a prime consideration.

When it comes to sustainability there is a balance. Most people want to do more to live an eco-friendly life, but they also want to make sure that it doesn't consume all of their time, energy, and money.

So how do you know where that balance is? How do you know if you're doing as much as you can do without dramatically changing the way you live your life?

Are You Ready to Take Sustainability to the Next Level?

Are You Ready for a Change?

Are You Looking to Feel More Fulfilled, Rewarded, and Engaged?

If you answered yes to any of these questions then you're ready to take sustainability to the next level. Don't worry; you don't have to go off the grid if you don't want to. Download this free book and you'll learn 8 different ideas to add more sustainable habits and projects to your life. Choose one or all eight – it's up to you. Visit the link below to download:

https://selfempowermentteam.com/sustainable-living

CHAPTER 6

Health & Nutrition

Keeping chickens means that you will have to become familiar with what they need to eat, the quantities, and any possible health-related issues they might develop. Though chickens are pretty self-reliant and low-maintenance, you may need to deal with the occasional injury and illness. Being informed about the signs to look out for that indicate your birds are under the weather will help you head off serious disasters. Chickens are quite resilient and can recover from just about any injury, if it is treated in time and appropriately. The following are some of the most important things to look out for and plan contingencies for.

Essentials for Raising Healthy Chickens

Chickens are what they eat. If they are confined to a small environment where they can only eat a limited diet that does not meet their needs, they will suffer and fall ill. For the dedicated chicken keeper, this is something to be avoided at all costs. Apart from the obvious animal cruelty implications, it will also affect the quality of your chickens' meat and create problems with their eggs and chicks. Even a feeding regimen that is lacking in only one essential element can have hugely detrimental effects on your flock.

- **Diet**

According to the Happychickencoop.com (2015), a balanced diet for backyard chickens is based on feeding high-quality poultry pellets. These pellets are made up of different quantities of wheat, salt, sunflower seed, maize, and oats. It is presented in an easily digestible format that your chickens will love and will greatly simplify the process of caring for your chickens. As an added bonus, these pellets have balanced quantities of vitamins, nutrients, and minerals that chickens would naturally get from sources such as digested soil, insects, fruits, and vegetables. If your chickens are kept cooped up, this ensures that they don't suffer any dietary deficiencies.

Like any animal, chickens can become bored with a meal, especially if it is all that they are given. One downside of feeding pellets only is that it removes the pleasure of watching your chickens peck and scratch in the dirt. So it is a good idea to supplement their diets with free grains such as maize (corn) crush or wheat that you can scatter at meal times for them to enjoy. You can and should include safe kitchen scraps for them to enjoy as well. These are a great way to boost the vitamin uptake in your chickens, thereby ensuring glossy feathers and limit any illnesses or diseases that your precious flock might develop from malnutrition. Kitchen scraps not only cut down on your feed bill, but it adds another link in sustainable living. As a bonus, your chickens will love you for it!

- **How Much To Feed**

Depending on the size of your chicken, the season, sex of the bird, and their overall health condition, you will need to adjust the feeding quantities of your chickens. In winter, you would feed more, while if you have hens you need to feed more than for roosters. If you have taken on a bird that is underweight you need to gradually increase their feed to avoid them gorging and rupturing their crop where they store food before digesting it in their gizzard.

Chickens have a unique digestive system, so overfeeding can be a real problem, especially with young chicks. Smaller sized bits are advisable, and you should take care to feed more regularly in smaller amounts, than a bumper meal once a day. Healthy chickens tend to self-regulate, but when you start, it's a good idea to err on the side of caution.

As a rule of thumb, you can quite safely give a medium-sized handful of pellets per chicken twice a day. An average hen will consume 1.5 pounds of feed per week, so that's a little less than a quarter-pound per day. You should keep an eye on your chickens after they have eaten. If they show signs of discomfort or look bloated, it may be an indication that they have been overfed, or that the size of the pellets are too large for them, if it's a smaller breed chicken. Pellets are available in smaller size chunks, which may be better either way.

When feeding, it is a good idea to use several feeding spots, or feeding stations as your chickens will have a pecking order. Using only one feeding place will lead to fighting and one or more chickens getting less food than the rest. Always ensure that there is sufficient water available. Chickens prefer drinking at ground level, so avoid high rimmed water feeders. Young chickens can also be clumsy, so don't use buckets of water that they may fall into and drown in.

When your hens are laying eggs, or are brooding on a clutch of eggs, it may be necessary for you to provide a special feed that is balanced to help them make up the calcium and protein loss that goes into the eggs. For hens brooding on their eggs, they will be spending approximately 21 days and will only rarely venture from their eggs. It may be kind to place a small amount of feed and water near the nest, to help her keep up her body weight and stay fed.

What to Feed or Not Feed

Apart from the balanced chicken feed pellets, you are encouraged to supplement your chickens' diet with scraps and treats. You may be concerned with what can be safely fed to your chickens, and what will improve their health. Always bear in mind that chickens are omnivores, and they will eat sometimes questionable foods that may not be good for their health, if not toxic. Some flowers are quite toxic to chickens, so it's a better idea to avoid feeding flowers. You could instead feed vegetable scraps, which are more nutritious and less harmful to your birds. It may be a little upsetting the first time that your chickens devour a juicy burger from McDonald's with gusto.

Cannibalism is quite prevalent among chickens, and they will happily gobble up bones, which are a rich source of calcium. To avoid future problems, it may be a better idea to let them peck at calcium sources such as oyster shells to avoid them turning on their own flock members. Ground-up eggshells are a good source of calcium, but to avoid them pecking at their own eggs, it is a wise practice to mash the eggs up so that they don't "identify" the shells as being eggs.

In some countries and states, it is illegal to feed certain scraps to chickens since these can spread diseases. Caution should be taken when feeding anything that is of an animal nature, so even though chickens will devour beef, poultry, sheep, pork, and fish, it is better to avoid these. Organically grown mealworms suitable for feeding to chickens can be ordered online, though other types are still illegal due to these worms being raised on animal proteins that could transfer diseases to your flock. A few juicy mealworms as a treat around molting time make for a great protein boost for your hens. However, free-ranging birds will happily chase down their own sources of proteins from spiders and moths to worms and crickets. They love eating plant lice as well and will help keep your garden louse free.

Vegetable kitchen scraps can be fed, if it is low in salts and sugars, which are bad for chickens. However, you should take care to only feed fresh scraps and remove whatever the chickens don't finish to avoid attracting flies. Leftover foods can also form mold, which is bad for your chickens and can lead to salmonella poisoning.

These vegetables, fruits, grains, and animal proteins are safe for chickens (thehappychickencoop.com, 2018).

Broccoli: High in vitamins, can be given cooked.

Tomatoes: Although a fruit, it is also considered a vegetable. Chickens love the tomato itself, but you should never give them the leaves or plant as this is highly toxic to chickens. The fruit is rich in vitamin C, K & B9 and also antioxidants.

Potatoes: You can give chickens raw or cooked potatoes or sweet potatoes, but not any sections that are green as this contains solanine, which is toxic. Never give them the leaves, stems, or flowers of the potato plant.

Cabbage: A big yes on this. It is loaded with trace minerals and vitamins that your chickens will love. As a bonus, you could hang the head of cabbage or place it in a wire cage that your chickens could play with to relieve boredom if they are cooped up.

Popcorn: A bit of a no-brainer, since popcorn is corn, which chickens love. Just ensure that there is no sugar, salt, or butter on. It is high in vitamins A, E & K. Your flock will love playing with the popped kernels.

Bananas: A lovely treat for hens as it's rich in vitamins B6, C & A and contains iron and magnesium to help with their general health. Again, you could tie up a few banana peels like little treasures along the chicken run to keep your chickens busy. Avoid feeding them green bananas though.

Apples: Chickens love apples due to the sweet taste. Any fruit should be given in moderation due to the rich sugar content. Fruit seeds are also indigestible to chickens and may be slightly toxic to them, so remove any seeds before feeding.

Cut grass: Your chickens will naturally peck away at your lawn if they have access. However, if they are in a coop or chicken run without access, you can supplement them by adding a few handfuls of untreated cut grass to their diet every other day. Make sure that the cuttings are fine to avoid their crops becoming tied up. The small seeds that grass forms in summer are a real treat to chickens.

Rice: Brown rice is best and rich in nutrients, however with any whole grain you should cook it before sharing with your chickens. Raw grains will soak up moisture in the chickens' digestive tracts and expand causing indigestion and even death. This is another reason why you should avoid feeding bread to young chickens. Traditionally, bread is fed to hens before slaughtering to fatten them up, but it can cause your chickens to tie up and die.

Crickets: You can purchase crickets online or from pet stores, and these are wonderful treats to brooding hens. At 12.9 grams of protein and 5.5 grams per 100 grams serving, they can help a chicken that is underweight to perk up quickly. You may need to feed this in moderation though to avoid getting overweight chickens, unless you plan on slaughtering them.

Berries: Chickens will love eating berries, but be careful considering the high sugar content, and the unexpected change in color of their droppings. Berries are rich in vitamins and antioxidants.

Pumpkin: This is an excellent nutritious source that is also entertaining for chickens. You could place a halved pumpkin (preferably a well-matured orange or yellow one) in their coop to keep them busy for several days. The seeds are also great at keeping your flock naturally worm-free.

Carrots: A big yes on this. If you have young chicks, you may need to rough dice this for them. Generally, chickens love carrots and will happily enjoy the foliage part too. It's a rich source of vitamins and minerals.

Oats: Raw or cooked oats are a stimulating treat for your chickens. Pullets also seem to respond well to it with a reduction in habits such as feather pecking. In winter, it is a great way to help warm up your flock by giving small amounts of warmed oatmeal to them. It should not be given too frequently though as the processed forms of oats that we buy from the shop tend to be slightly congestive to the chicken crop.

Cauliflower stems: Chickens love this, and it is a nutritious snack. They aren't really interested in the heads though.

Salads: You can feed most leftover scraps of salads, however, remember that it has likely been seasoned with salts that are bad for your chickens. It would be better to feed scraps before adding spices and salts to your salads. Chickens love pecking at lettuce and even cucumber pieces. Peppers tend to not be a favorite among chickens, and the plants are toxic, so avoid it.

Corn on the cob: Since it's corn, your chickens will love pecking at a cut cob after or before you have de-pipped it. Just be careful of the usual added salts and butter that people put on corn cobs, which may be harmful to your chickens.

Quinoa: a wonderfully nutritious grain, though given the cost, it may not end up as scrap. Avoid bread, even if it contains quinoa, as bread is generally not suited to chickens and molds quickly.

Garlic: The verdict is still out on this, however, chickens seem to love garlic flakes and even raw garlic plants. Some believe that too much will taint the taste of the hen's eggs, but it is a natural immune booster and will help keep worms away. A good idea to feed in moderation.

Fish: Chickens love fish. They enjoy the flesh, bones, and intestines. It is a rich source of protein and calcium, and as a bonus, it has less potential to contain transferable diseases that are associated with feeding other forms of animal proteins to your chickens. Many agricultural stores sell fish-meal as a natural additive to chicken feeds.

There are a few foods that you should avoid feeding your chickens at all costs. These usually contain toxic chemicals that will quickly kill off your flock. Your chickens will happily gobble these up, should they come up on the menu, so you should take care not to let your chickens have access to your garbage bin.

Processed foods: Avoid feeding your chickens baked or preserved goods such as muffins, cakes, cookies, pasta, pizza, and pickled foods. They are rich in sugar and salts and contain no nutrients for your flock. Since they will swell up on contact with your chicken's digestive juices, they could also lead to a blocked digestive tract.

Salt rich foods: Vegetable crisps, seafood that has added salt, chips, and popcorn with salt are a really bad idea. Apart from the additives in vegetable crisps and chips, the salt will create an electrolyte imbalance in your chickens, which will result in their hearts stopping.

Moldy foods: Never feed your chickens anything that is past the best by date and has started molding. Molds have a highly toxic chemical content for chickens. When buying your chicken feed pellets, you should also check the date of manufacture and smell the food to check that it hasn't been exposed to moisture and begun molding.

Caffeine rich foods such as teas and coffee: These contain caffeine which is highly toxic to chickens. Rather enjoy your cuppa as you watch your flock happily scratching at their safe snacks.

Foods sprayed with pesticides: Chickens have a robust, but sensitive digestive tract, and you should avoid feeding them anything that has been chemically treated.

Chickens will love most types of vegetables. Avoid vegetables that are under-ripe such as green potatoes or green tomatoes. Since they don't have teeth, you may also need to cut the veggies into manageable sizes for them, or dice it with one or two pulses in the food processor. Greedy chickens do choke, so avoid those odd sizes that they will gulp down, but be unable to digest; instead, go for fine slices. Image: Sven Scheuermeier on Unsplash.

Common Illnesses and Treatments

There are a number of illnesses that can plague your flock, and some of them can become dangerous to you and your family too. Starting on the outside of the chicken, there are a number of parasitic organisms that could invade your chickens, according to thehappychickencoop.com (2019):

Mites: These can be difficult to spot given their small size, and their nasty habit of hiding in the feathers. Though small, a heavy mite load can literally suck your chickens dry as mites are blood feeders. They will find a soft place to settle and feed on your chickens like little vampires, until your chicken becomes anemic. In extreme cases, your chickens could even die. As with all parasites, the old and young are especially vulnerable. Signs of your chicken having an infestation could be over-preening and unseasonal feather loss. Some mites love targeting the fleshy, blood-rich areas around the chicken's eyes, beak, and comb. If you have keen eyes, you might see them like black dust that seems to cling to your birds. If the infestation is really bad, your chickens will suffer blood loss, and their bright red combs will be pale in color.

Chickens will naturally dust bathe to keep their mites under control, but in extreme cases, you may need to help them out with a commercial product such as Sevin 5%, which will help kill off any unwanted residents on your chickens.

Some mites, such as the red mite, live not on your chicken, but in their coop. These tenacious mites feed at night, and a sure sign of a possible infestation could be your chickens being reluctant to roost at night. In extreme cases, you may need to build a new coop and burn the old one as these mites can be really difficult to get rid of.

The last type of mite prevalent in the Northern U.S. is the scaly leg mite. It lives in and around the scales on your chicken's legs. They cause the scales to become dry, lift, and flake off. This can be painful and can cause your chickens to become lame, even turning sickly and dying. Dusting your chickens will help, but an old-wives remedy works even better. You start by soaking the chicken's legs in warm water to soften any dry scales and remove debris. Then you coat the legs with olive oil, rub off any excess, and finally coat the legs with Vaseline to smother the mites and any eggs.

If your chickens have been suffering from mites for a while and are sickly, you may need to adjust their diets to fight off the effects of anemia. Adding poultry nutri drench to your chicken's water may be good and feeding a protein-rich feed for a while such as game bird feed may help restore your chicken's natural balance.

Bed Bugs: Another external parasite to guard against is bedbugs, and these can easily infest your coop and your chickens' laying boxes. Therefore, you should clean your coop regularly and use good quality poultry dust to treat the area, as well as providing fresh hay for your chickens to nest in. Bed Bugs also live off blood meals.

Fleas and Lice: Chickens, like other domestic birds, are prone to getting fleas. Sometimes the fleas live in the manure, and other flea species live in the feathers. As with most parasites, they live on blood meals. Dusting your chickens, their coop and cleaning the area of manure is a good practice to get into. You can also use diatomaceous earth to dust the area with, and your chickens may also ingest some of this, which is said to be a natural dewormer and antiparasitic.

Flies and Mosquitoes: Chickens are as bothered by these two pests as humans. These blood feeders are drawn to the chickens' blood-rich combs and legs where they can cause real misery. It is a good idea to keep water feeders clean of standing water, and you should clean the coop regularly to remove any excess manure and leftover feed that might attract flies. As an added concern, mosquitoes can cause avian pox in chickens, so you may need to vaccinate your birds if you live in an area that is rife with mozzies. Another fly species that can cause real problems are blowflies. Though they don't actually feed off your chickens, they can lay their eggs in the soft flesh of the chickens. The soft and moist flesh of the area under your hens is especially susceptible. Treating this can be a time-consuming process as the resulting maggots need to be removed by hand. The area is then treated with hydrogen peroxide to discourage reinfestation and then sprayed with poultry approved wound spray.

With parasites, prevention is better than cure. Always ensure that your chickens have a clean, well-dusted environment in which to live. When dusting the coop, keep your chickens in a separate cage to prevent them from breathing in too much dust. If you are dusting a chicken for mites or lice, you should take care not to dust the beak area too vigorously to prevent them from inhaling the dust.

Having considered the external parasites, we should now look at the numerous diseases that your chickens can develop. Chicks are the most susceptible to diseases, and these can be introduced into your flock with a new chicken that has not been quarantined or comes from an unregistered breeder. Fortunately, there are signs to look for and vaccinations are available for many diseases. You may need to consult with a veterinarian to administer a vaccine, or treat your pet chicken with hospitalization if they're severely affected. Worst case scenario, you may need to cull members of your flock to safeguard the other birds. Lakesidefeed.com (2019) covers some of the common illnesses that may hurt your flock.

Infectious Bronchitis: Much like the common cold in humans, this can lead to mass deaths if not treated. The symptoms are the same as in humans with nasal discharge, watery eyes, and sneezing. If you are using an artificial brooder, you can raise the temperature slightly, and feed warmed, moist mash that helps the chicks eat and digest their food better. There is no cure, much like in humans, and the chicks will have to recover on their own. You can help them by providing antibiotics to prevent secondary infection. Infected birds should be isolated from the rest of the flock to prevent the rest of your chickens from becoming infected.

Rot Gut: Chicks suffering from severe diarrhea may have fallen prey to this bacterial infection that is rife in overcrowded brooding machines or poorly cleaned coops. The chicks become depressed and feed poorly, resulting in death. An antibiotic can be ordered from your vet to add to their drinking water.

Aspergillosis: This is a respiratory disease that is caused by a fungus, again in overcrowded brooders or poorly cleaned coops. It is incredibly important to keep a well maintained and planned chicken operation. Overcrowding leads to many diseases that your chicks will fall prey to first.

Fowl Pox: A particularly nasty disease spread by mosquitoes that affect birds by creating wart-like growths on their bodies. It negatively affects chick growth, and the only cure is to treat with vaccinations and keep the area mosquito-free.

Marek's Disease: Another respiratory disease that can have symptoms such as paralysis and blindness in chicks. It's usually fatal. If this has begun rearing its ugly head among your chicks you may need to vaccinate your brood as soon as possible. Overcrowding is widely held as one of the causes of the spread of this disease.

Avian Encephalomyelitis: Sadly, this is a 100 percent fatal disease, and affected chicks will have to be destroyed as soon as they are noticed. There are vaccines available to prevent this if it seems to be prevalent in your area, or if you have had a chick present with the symptoms, which include dull eyes, paralysis, shaking heads, and loss of appetite. This is usually spread through feces contaminated feeds and overcrowding.

If you decide to rear chicks, it is very important to inspect them daily to ensure that they are healthy. They have a very low tolerance for illness, so you should take action immediately if you notice a chick being under the weather. To prevent mass death among your chicks you should isolate any affected chicks and double up your regular checks for any symptoms such as weakness, loss of appetite, weight loss, and diarrhea. Ensure that all chicks are kept warm, but well ventilated. Avoid overcrowding which will compound any illness and lead to mass deaths.

Common Injuries and Treatments

If you are now wondering what else can possibly go wrong with your fledgling flock of beautiful hens, chicks, and roosters, there is one more terror to discuss. Injuries. Yes, chickens are injury-prone. Chicks especially are often booted out of the coop by other chickens, bitten by dogs, get their delicate feet caught in obstructions, and can easily suffer the amputation of a limb and topical infections. Here are some common chicken injuries that most chicken keepers have to deal with on a daily basis, according to Mormino (n.d.).

Predator strikes: Chickens can suffer severe injuries from bites and claw punctures, and can have internal injuries from being shaken around by animals such as a dog clamping its jaws and shaking the chicken. Falcons swooping in can inflict deep and painful punctures with their talons.

Dogs have a natural hunting instinct, so don't be surprised if even a lap dog takes the opportunity to try to catch, slay, and eat your chickens. The injuries caused by dog bites can range from broken feathers, puncture wounds, and broken legs, to horrendous tears. Image: James Barker on Unsplash.

- **Conflict within the flock**: Chickens have a pecking order, and they can be extremely vicious on their own kind. Chicks often suffer pecking injuries at the hands of other hens, who recognize that the chick is not their own and therefore they attack it. Hens and roosters will often fight against other chickens to establish their dominance. This could result in serious peck marks, scratches from talons–remember that roosters and even some older hens can develop scarily ferocious spurs that have no problem slicing flesh–and chickens may face this daily. Hens often suffer abuse from overzealous roosters who can pluck them to pieces while mating. This can be seen as a loss of feathers along the back where the rooster grabs on and kicks in with those spurs.

- **Occasional injuries**: Chicks are not extremely mobile, and they can easily become tangled up in something such as an old net, or even a tree branch. This can result in injuries ranging from bruising to cuts and even a foot being ripped off. Even older chickens can be injured in strange and haphazard ways. This is why you should inspect your birds on a daily basis. These injuries are often hidden away in the mass of feathers, and over time a minor injury can become serious if not treated in time.

It is advisable to keep a chicken care kit ready in advance, rather than notice an injury on a Sunday night, and then need to find supplies that are not available from your local seven-eleven. These are some basics to keep on hand to treat injuries with:

Gauze, bandages, ice-cream sticks, vetericyn eyewash and vetericyn wound treatment, povidone iodine solution (betadine), sterile syringes, vitamin or electrolyte supplement, Meloxicam or aspirin, old towels to wrap an injured bird in, warm water bottles, and an extra cage or safe container to isolate an injured bird in (a pet carrier can also be helpful).

When preparing to treat your first injured chicken, it is important not to become emotional–even if it's your dear and loved pet chicken. Your chicken will need you to be calm, even if it looks like they have been put through a meat grinder. You need to calmly immobilize the injured bird, and then carefully assess the extent of the damage. Bear in mind that chickens are blood rich animals–it will probably look more serious than it may actually be.

Given that there will be blood everywhere, you need to clean the area with water, stop any constant bleeding with a firmly applied gauze pad held in place for a while. If the bleeding continues excessively it may mean that the chicken has suffered damage of a vascular nature, and you should consider taking it to a vet. If the bleeding slows down, you may be able to save your chicken by taping a dressing in place. Before doing this though, you need to effectively clean the area with a wound wash. If there are any broken feathers or bits of dead skin that may interfere with the healing process you will need to pluck these or cut off what will possibly bother the dressing. Don't pull out pinions though as they have a heavy blood supply, and you don't want to add to your woes by dealing with a pinion injury too.

Having dressed the wound, you then need to keep the chicken warm and if necessary administer a solution of electrolytes to ward off shock. Keeping them immobile and wrapped in a towel is a good idea. Remove them from the flock as other chickens will peck at wounds and can even become attracted to the smell of an injured bird. Don't be surprised if your flock finishes off one of its own that has been injured. After all, chickens can easily resort to cannibalism at the hint of an injured coop mate. Instead, keep the injured bird in a separate cage or box to minimize the risk of an additional injury. Depending on the severity of the chicken's shock and the weather, you may need to add warm water bottles (or gel warming pads) to the towel to help your chicken deal with shock. Avoid bright lights that could further traumatize your chicken.

Assess the possibility of your chicken being in pain. If they have suffered a serious bite, or lost part of a foot, broken a leg, or lost a toe, they will probably be in quite a bit of pain–surely you would be too, if it happened to you? It is appropriate to administer pain medicine via syringe. Meloxicam is a brilliant anti-inflammatory medicine that is prescribed to most animals at different potencies. Make sure that you have the type suited for chickens, as you can't use the same potency given to dogs for instance. Your vet can advise you on the quantities and frequencies at which to administer this. In a pinch, you can also use aspirin to help with pain relief. You can add five tablets of aspirin to one gallon of water and offer this as drinking water to the injured bird. However, do not offer aspirin if there is the chance that the bird has suffered internal injuries as aspirin is a blood thinner and will result in the chicken bleeding to death. With external injuries, you can control the bleeding by applying pressure dressings. As a rule of thumb, you should always be able to insert one finger slightly between any dressing and the chicken's body to avoid completely cutting off blood flow to the affected area.

Once your chicken survives the initial shock, you will have to assess a further treatment plan. Open wounds need to be treated with antibiotic creams and regular wound treatment with vetericyn. Keep an eye for signs of infection such as red and swollen flesh. Watch out for the chicken pecking at its own injuries. Keep the bird hydrated with an electrolyte solution, but don't do this for more than three days as your bird could develop heart problems as a result. In severe cases, you may need to feed the bird a liquid diet to keep its strength up, and it is advisable to feed a warm mash with small particles to help digestion. Don't overdo the force-feeding, though you can help a traumatized bird with the occasional syringe of mash. When force-feeding, take care to avoid clogging the nostrils as chickens have a delicate respiratory system. You can check on the bird's "fullness" by feeling the crop with your finger. Never feed to the point that the crop becomes hard to the touch.

When dealing with injuries such as severed toes, feet, and other severe lacerations, you need to offer support to the chicken while it heals and recovers. Chickens can heal quite well from injuries such as broken legs, lost toes, and cuts to appendages such as the wattle or comb. Taping a support of ice-cream sticks to a broken leg can help the chicken heal effectively, as long as you can keep the limb clean and well dressed.

During your chicken's stay in the recovery cage or box, you need to ensure that your chicken has soft bedding and that the area is kept clean of feces, which may cause secondary infections. Upon returning the healed chicken to the coop, you should keep in mind that your recovered chicken has been absent and has lost its place in the pecking order. It is like introducing a new chicken to your flock all over again. Perhaps keep the chicken in an isolated cage where the other chickens can socialize through the mesh for a day or two. Once they have had a chance to settle, you could then reintroduce your chicken back into the poultry population. With some luck and sustained effort, you can save most of your chickens from illness, mishaps, and injuries. Chickens are really quite resilient, and when they feel less terrified, their chances of healing are dramatically improved. Sadly, not all chickens make it.

Handling Chicken Deaths

At some point, you will suffer the loss of chickens from your backyard coop. It is an inevitable truth, and despite the lengths that you go through to save a beloved chicken pet, you may be faced with the point of euthanizing your chicken. It is advisable to find a caring vet that is willing to do this for you before such an event happens. Some chicken owners become proficient with manual euthanizing of chickens. In layman's terms, this procedure known as cervical dislocation is known as "breaking its neck." If correctly applied, it is quick and painless.

If your chicken is euthanized by your vet, they usually offer a disposal service for the remains. However, if your chicken has died at home, or you chose to perform a cervical dislocation at home, you will become responsible for the remains. It is extremely important not to simply place a dead chicken in the trash, and it certainly can't go to the pot–if you were breeding chickens for slaughter. Ill or injured chickens are a health hazard. They should be kept away from other chickens, pets, and people. Birds treated with antibiotics also have a withdrawal period, so even if they have recovered and then die a few days or even a week later, they will not be suitable for consumption. Therefore, once the chicken has died, you should at the very least bury it at a depth of two or more feet. Be careful not to bury the chicken near a water source such as a pond or stream as the microbes contained in the remains can pollute water, spreading disease to other animals. In winter the ground may be too hard to dig a hole, and it is suggested that you make contact with your local vet or animal shelter that regularly deals with euthanasia of pets to find a safe way to dispose of chicken remains.

Your chickens will enjoy healthy lives if you take care to give them appropriate feed and avoid overcrowding them. You should ensure that their coops, runs, nesting boxes, and free-range areas are well cleaned to avoid diseases proliferating. By monitoring your little flock you can become alerted to problems while they are just starting, and you can then still do something to stave off disaster. Illnesses, parasites, and injuries should be dealt with swiftly as there is no excuse for an animal to suffer. Should your chicken survive due to your interventions, you will find them to be grateful creatures, and many chicken breeders have had a broken-legged chick become a favored pet that happily hobbled along in their shadow for many years.

CHAPTER 7

Eggcellent Eggs

Many of us dream of having those freshly laid eggs at our disposal on a daily basis. It would be even better if the hens could lay them all in a neat tray on the back porch every morning. However, this is not likely to happen, and it may take some work to get a system in place where you can collect eggs every morning with a minimal amount of fuss. Ensuring a steady supply of eggs is all about knowing how much to feed, when to feed, what to feed, and knowing your chickens' unique body language. If you build a good relationship with your hens, then gathering the eggs will not be as arduous a task as you might think.

Having fresh eggs in a steady supply is a wonderful part of sustainable living. You will be amazed at the sizes, shapes, colors, and textures that your hens will produce eggs in. Eggs are not only good to eat, but they can also be a source of excitement as you see which hen has produced daily, or wait for a clutch to hatch. Either way, they are great fun for the whole family. Image: Rebekah Howell on Unsplash.

Essential Knowledge

When your hens start laying eggs you will need to supplement their diet by feeding them a broodmix feed pellet, which is higher in protein to help them produce quality eggs. As with any animal that is producing offspring, you need to increase their calcium uptake, so you can also feed them crushed oyster shells. As a bonus, this will also improve the hardness of the eggshells, thereby improving the overall health of the eggs. A laying hen will also eat more, so you need to feed her up to four ounces of feed per day to keep her well enough to produce eggs.

Another bonus is that your hens will announce loudly that a fresh egg has just been delivered, usually in the morning. Some hens lay throughout the day, so you can also check in the afternoon. An average hen will lay about an egg a day when she starts going into a laying cycle. Luckily, the eggs will keep perfectly well for you to collect later that day, as long as you don't have an egg eater in the coop. That's right, chickens like eggs as much as we do. Some chickens quickly learn to peck at their neighbor's eggs and sadly this behavior can't be unlearned. If you have an egg-eating chicken in the coop, you may need to keep it isolated from the other hens to prevent this from happening. It is also a good idea to pick up any broken eggs quickly to prevent a chicken from picking up this unfortunate habit.

Eggs really are nature's perfect blessing and they come with their own natural packaging that not only keeps them fresh for quite a while, but also keeps in nutrients and keeps out bacteria. A glossy layer, called a bloom, is present around all freshly laid eggs. So, you should avoid washing eggs when you have collected them. Rather wipe them clean, and store them in a cool place, especially if you have fertilized eggs. If you do have to wash them, you could wipe them with a good quality vegetable oil to ensure that they stay fresh. This is what many commercial egg producers do. If your eggs are really fresh, the shell may still be quite soft. That's okay, it will harden upon continued contact with the air.

If you have forgotten when your eggs were laid, you can easily check on the freshness by doing the water test. Simply place the egg in a bowl of water. Use enough water to submerge the egg. If the egg lies on its side at the bottom you have a fresh egg. If the egg floats end to the top, it is starting to lose freshness, while an egg that floats to the top is bound to be a smelly and nasty surprise.

Behavior, Gathering, and Shortages

When gathering eggs, it is a good idea to keep them in marked containers that allow you to keep the date on them. This is an effective way to track which eggs were laid when. Eggs will keep at least a month in the refrigerator. For the most part, a hen that is laying eggs, will be quite happy to leave the nest to feed. This is a good opportunity to gather an egg or two. However, once a hen has laid several eggs, she might become really broody and start "sticking" to the nest. Not even the promise of a meal will get her to budge and you may need to be quite forceful to gather eggs then. A brooding hen will peck at any threat that approaches her nest–including a roving hand. It is a good idea to wear heavy-duty leather gloves to protect your hands in that case. When approaching the nest, the idea is not to startle the hens or frighten them. You want them to keep laying in that nest, so don't shoo them off the nest. With the protection of some sturdy gloves, you can quite safely reach under the hen's fluffy bottom and pull out the egg from the nest. Older hens that are used to this will quite happily let you get in there to collect eggs. A hen that feels threatened will look for another place to lay her eggs, in which case, you may not find the eggs in time to use them. Hens will nest in anything from an old bucket and a hay bale to a not-so-convenient downpipe. Therefore, it is best to keep the collection process as trauma-free as possible. Keep this in mind when you train your children to fetch eggs.

It is not a good idea to let a hen sit on a clutch of fertile eggs, unless you are planning to let her hatch them. Once a hen has begun brooding on those eggs, they quickly enter the maturation process and taking those eggs for cooking can yield some unpleasant results. The chicks develop quite quickly in the egg. With both fertilized and unfertilized eggs, you should gather them daily to ensure that they are fresh and suitable for eating. A fertilized egg that is being brooded, either by a brooding machine or a hen, will hatch in approximately 21 days.

Most egg shortages will happen in the winter months as hens are triggered by the change in light to slow the production of eggs. If you want to maintain a steady supply of eggs all year round, then you could consider installing a lighting and warming system in your coop that better simulates natural lighting conditions to trick your hens into laying eggs. A system that runs on a 12-hour timer is best. This is how the massive factory farms go about it. To ensure that your eggs still follow nature's process and is rich in nutrition, keep your lighting system as close to the normal summer lighting cycle as possible. There are breeds of chickens that are good layers despite the colder months and changes in the lighting cycle. So if you live way up north, you may have to keep hens suited to those conditions.

Most pullets will start laying eggs at 18 to 20 weeks of age. They are only considered a fully-fledged hen after a year. For hens to continue laying eggs, they need a full

12 hours of daylight. Hens will lay quite consistently up to the age of two to three years, and after that, they will lay occasionally. Some reports suggest that though they lay less, they produce larger eggs then. At this point, you will have to consider whether you will replace the hen, earmark her for the pot, or keep her as a pet. Either way, if you need eggs, you will have to invest in a younger hen. Your local laws might become a problem if you want to keep an old hen and get in a new hen—you could quickly end up with several more chickens than is legally allowed.

One benefit of an older hen is that she makes a great brooding machine. If you plan to eat some eggs and hatch others, you can easily keep every other egg in the nesting box for your older hen to hatch. Older hens also seem better at raising chicks than younger pullets are. A brooding hen will not be able to lay as consistently if she is sitting on a clutch of eggs. Remember that the hen will stick to roughly a 21-day cycle, and she will not keep laying eggs too long after the cycle for hatching begins. This makes sense as the hen will not want a clutch of fully hatched eggs, half-hatched, and freshly laid eggs as she will want to begin leading the chicks around to feed. To ensure consistent egg laying, you should remove the eggs daily.

If you are aiming at hatching a clutch of eggs, it is interesting to know that research has proven there is communication between the embryos and the hen, and there even seems to be evidence that the embryos will communicate with each other with later laid eggs speeding up their incubation process to meet the hatching "deadline" (Jacob, n.d.).

Young hens, or pullets, will prefer to nest on the floor. If your nesting boxes are high up, you might end up with hens laying eggs on the floor, which could lead to egg eating behavior among the rest of the flock. To know when a hen is getting ready to start laying, you will notice that she begins to examine the laying boxes or out-of-the-way areas that may serve as a nesting box. The hen will be quite restless and sit in possible nesting boxes for longer periods as she prepares the nest with her body molding the straw or hay. At times, older hens may peck at younger pullets to prevent them from nesting, in which case, you could end up with the young hen having to lay her egg on the ground. You should then move the younger hen to a separate nesting box to encourage her to lay eggs without being bullied by the older hens. It may help to initially move the laid egg to a nest and confine the hen there for a few hours to give her an opportunity to build her own nest. This should ensure that the young hen lays her following eggs in a nest. If you are struggling with roving egg layers, then it is best to keep your hens confined to the coop for the early morning as this is the time that they will most naturally lay eggs.

Hens have an urge to fill an empty nesting box with eggs, so don't leave eggs in the nest if you plan on having a steady supply of eggs. When you have young hens that have never laid before, you can even train them to use the nesting boxes for laying eggs. It's a good idea to use a golf ball for this as it seems to hint at them to add their own eggs to this "egg." However, don't use a real egg to train them as they will likely just end up pecking at the egg and this will cause egg-eating behavior.

It is a reality that some hens are just not suited to laying a constant supply of eggs, and you should keep in mind that you get what you pay for. If you want a quality egg producer, you should purchase your pullets from a recognized breeder that has a history of breeding hens that produce. This may cost quite a bit more than you had initially budgeted for. Bear in mind though that you can defray some of this cost by raising quality chicks and selling eggs. So, once your eggs have hatched, you are ready to enjoy the wonderful world of chicks!

CHAPTER 8

Baby Chicks

Chicks are a true delight to watch, hold, and raise. They offer a wonderful connection to nature and allow your children to learn about where food comes from and the importance of our actions upon animals to ensure that

food supply. When properly cared for, chicks have a high survival rate and will add value to your lives as chickens for slaughter or future egg layers. Image: Daniel Tuttle on Unsplash.

Now that your coop is ready, you may receive chicks in one of two ways. You can either order day-old chicks from a registered breeder, or your existing hens will begin hatching chicks for you. When you are expecting chicks, there are a few things to take cognizance of and a few must-haves to invest in to ensure that your chicks have the best chance in life.

Before Your Chicks Arrive

If you are getting day-old chicks from a hatchery or chicken breeder, you will need to invest in a brooder beforehand. Young chicks need to keep warm consistently, and this may mean some effort will be required on your part. You need to ensure that a red brooder lamp is installed in a draft-free mini-coop for the chicks. They are quite susceptible to changes in temperature, so having a spare lamp is a must. If you only have a few chicks, you can help them stay warm in this brooder by adding a feather duster placed upside down to simulate the hen's body. Mostly, the chicks will be quite happy in their brooder, pecking away at starter feeds and sipping water. Initially, you need to keep a close eye on the chicks to ensure that they don't have any diseases or problems. Some chicks will need encouragement to drink, and if they are ill, you will need to add certain medicines to their drinking water. If you have a chick that is not looking strong, and you suspect illness, it is advisable to separate it from the rest of the brood. This is where having a second brooding lamp can become very useful.

If your hens have hatched chicks, you will have to be equally diligent. You need to monitor the chicks for their health. And if it is necessary, you need to remove ill chicks and keep them in a separate brooder to heal. Risking infection of all the chicks is simply not worth it. Ensure that you regularly feed the chicks in small amounts, as chicks can easily gorge themselves and rupture their crops. When there is more than one hen with a clutch of chicks, you may need to watch out for bullying, fighting, and injuries. In small coups, hens can fight over resources for their chicks. Again, having a smaller mobile cage to keep a belligerent hen and her clutch in could be helpful.

Remember, your chicks will be a much smaller and weaker version of the adult chickens. This means that you will have to check the coop for holes that they could escape from, check your yard for places they could fall into or get stuck in, and guard against any local predators that might make a quick meal out of a little fluffy bundle. Chicks drown very easily, so watch that your waterers are not deep and threatening to the new chicks. Also, check that the chicks can reach the waterers to drink. This might mean placing a few ice-cream tub lids around with water in for very small chicks. If your coop is a multi-story construction, you also need to ensure that the chicks don't fall off the ramp and injure themselves. Adding some temporary plastic sheeting or sponge to keep them on the ramp will help prevent injuries.

If you are in a particularly cold climate, you may need to combine hay and sawdust bedding to create warm nests for the hen to snuggle with her chicks at night. Be careful, though, to get dust-free pine shavings as chicks have a very sensitive respiratory system. When dusting the coop, you should also do so very lightly when the chicks are still very small. Wait until the dust has settled, so to speak, before returning the chicks to the coop between cleanings.

Caring For Chicks

Brooder chicks are quite a bit more work as you need to become a surrogate mom for your chicks. You will have to check on them, teach them to drink, monitor that they eat and poop, as well as keep them warm. Unfortunately, most hens will not foster pre-hatched chicks. Instead, they will likely kill them upon sight. If you have a hen brooding already on some eggs, and you have just bought eggs that are almost ready to hatch, you could sneak one or two eggs in among her clutch. Should they hatch with the rest, the hen will probably raise the foster chicks along with her own clutch.

In a brooder, you will have to use good quality sawdust as a bed, and ensure that there is a regular starter feed and water supply. Chicks, unlike other farm babies, may need to be taught to drink water. With the hen, they will learn by copying the mother's behavior. Initially, you may need to gently push their beaks into some water and help them raise their beaks up to swallow the fluid. Chickens have a cleft palate, which means they can't create suction to actually suck up fluids. They have to take a mouthful and then raise their beaks to quaff down the liquid. It is quite adorable to watch them drinking, so you can teach your kids about helping the chicks in the beginning.

Hens are naturally protective of their chicks so be warned. If your children want to handle the chicks, you should teach them how to do so with respect. Children can easily hurt a chick, or cause it to become ill if it is shaken or kept from the hen for too long. Image: Ro Han on Pexels.com.

Your children will want to hold the chicks frequently, and this will require some supervision until they know how and when to hold the chicks. Chickens are not puppies and can't be rolled onto their backs to hold. A chicken's lungs are located just below it's back, so lying on the back could lead to breathing problems. Additionally, a chicken has a complex digestive system and being upended can cause the crop to become upset. Diarrhea is a sure sign that the chick is being over-handled. With chicks that have been hatched by the hen, it is important not to handle them too much, as the chicks need to bond with and follow the hen. She is the one who will protect and teach her chicks. Don't be surprised if a sweet-natured hen turns into a hellcat when she has a clutch hiding under her wings.

In a brooder, chicks will be kept at 92 degrees Fahrenheit, and this will be reduced by five degrees per week once the chicks start feathering. At six weeks' age, or if they are well covered, robust, and the weather is warm, you can introduce them to the flock and the coop. At this point, you can also take them off the starter feed and switch to grower mash. It may be a good idea to slowly change their diet by feeding a mix of half-half each feed type for the first week that they are in the coop.

Hens and their broods will rely on you to supply a starter feed for the young chicks, and you should take care to feed a hen with her chicks separately from the older chickens. A baby chick's crop is not designed to eat a large-sized pellet, and though you may find it amusing to watch the chick gobble down some large pellets, a dead chick later on will be less amusing. Watch the chicks for any sign of pecking on their bodies. For some reason, perhaps due to the pecking instinct, chickens will peck at anything–even freckles on a child's face–so be warned. A slightly bloodied chick will become a target to the other chickens, and they will eagerly peck it to death.

Young chicks may also seem disoriented at times, and though it's less likely to happen under the hen's care, they may snuggle up in corners of the coop and end up suffocating. So, block off corners with some tightly rolled feed bags or extra mesh to discourage them from this. In your brooder, you need to take care of any corners and do likewise. Chicks that constantly wander away from the hen need to be carefully monitored for signs of disease or malnutrition. A weak chick is an easy target for both illness and parasites.

By appropriately handling a young chick you can accustom it to being treated for illness, dusting for parasites, and treating injuries. Chickens are quite happy to adjust to the demands of their home environment, and they will easily become tamed enough for your children to handle responsibly.

Chick Development

Chicks begin as a fertilized disc on the egg yolk known as the germinal disc. The eggs are fertilized 24 hours before the egg is laid. Once laid, an egg can enter a period of stasis where it is not developing. This is required for the hen to lay several eggs that can then be brooded on together. Hence, a hen that is brooding might take several days to lay a full clutch of 12 to 14 eggs. As previously mentioned, the hen communicates with the embryos, and the eggs laid last will speed up their development process to meet the hatching "deadline."

Between the 18th and 21st days of development, the chick will consume the last of the protein-rich egg yolk, thereby finding the strength to hatch and survive for several days without really eating after it is hatched, as it learns to eat and drink. The chick will use the egg-tooth (the small hook that newborn chicks have on their beaks) to make a break through the internal sack within the egg into the air pocket that is found inside the egg. At this point, the chick will begin to chirp within the egg. The hatching process is completed by the chick cracking the eggshell with the egg-tooth. The chick then breaks out of the egg (4H Virtual Farm, n.d.).

Chicks go through various developmental stages to become a fully matured hen or rooster. Within the first week of hatching, a chick will begin to grow feathers. Most of the downy coating that chicks are born with will have disappeared within five weeks. Chicks require a lot more feed as they grow, and they will feed all day and all night long, as long as the lights are on. Soon, your chicks will reach that gangly stage when their feathers seem to not suit their long and lanky bodies, like a girl with a dress that shrunk.

At times it can be difficult to tell what sex the chicks are, unless they are bred to reveal their sex with a certain coloring, and this can make it difficult to decide which birds to keep and which to sell. One theory, though not scientific, is that when you press down on the young chick's head, if the tail lifts, it's a hen. If it doesn't, it's a rooster. The jury is still out on the success of this way to predict the sex of chicks. Scientifically speaking, roosters tend to grow thicker legs and grow taller than pullets, which grow larger bodies. The real proof is when the pullet begins nesting, or the young rooster starts that awkward crowing that your neighbors will "love." A maturing hen will also get in the habit of squatting down when a rooster approaches, signaling that she's ready to start breeding.

Introducing Chicks to the Flock

Introducing chicks to the coop can be a challenging event, especially if they have been hatched and raised in a brooder. For one, they will not have a hen that will protect them. It is also not advisable to introduce a solitary chick to the flock. In that case, you need to wait until the chick is almost fully grown to allow it to have the strength and resilience to face up to the "farm yard bullies." It is a better idea to introduce the whole clutch of chicks as they can stick together and help each other stay warm, as well as divide the attention of the other chickens so that one chick doesn't get isolated and pecked on.

You should wait until your brooder chicks are at least six weeks old before introducing the chicks to the coop. If the weather is still somewhat cold at night, you may need to catch the chicks every afternoon and return them to the brooder for the night until they have developed more feathers. It will also be a good idea to have certain areas of your coop closed off with large mesh, that the chicks can fit through, but that will keep the larger chickens at bay to give your chicks a safe place to hide. Remember to provide water and starter feed for the chicks in a safe place where they can eat without being harassed by the older chickens.

Initially, you need to ensure that the chicks do not have access to the feeds meant for the older chickens, as the extra calcium in layer feeds are not suitable for young chicks. It's okay for the older chickens to be on growers mash for a while, though feeding oyster shells will be a good idea too.

Chick Problems

The most common problems with chicks, that can cause death, are when they contract any of the illnesses that were covered in chapter six. Injuries are also something to keep an eye on, especially when they have entered the flock. However, some other problems to be prepared for can also crop up (Mormino, n.d.):

- **Dehydration**

As mentioned, chicks absorb the rich yolk of their eggs before hatching, and this means that they don't need to eat or drink for two to three days after hatching. Nature intended it this way to enable the whole clutch to hatch before the hen takes her chicks exploring and teaches them about feeding and drinking. This also enables large hatcheries to sell chicks by mail and courier service. They keep well in a ventilated box for a day or two until they reach their destination. However, chicks can arrive at the new yard suffering from dehydration and may have begun starving. Once they have arrived, you should encourage them to start drinking immediately. If a chick is particularly weak or heat strained, you can help them along by syringing small quantities of water and electrolyte solution into their beaks, should they refuse to drink on their own. A little water goes a long way, so don't force down large quantities as it may have an adverse reaction.

- **Pasted Vent**

This is an often neglected condition that should be treated immediately. It occurs when a chick has a build-up of feces that sticks to the vent area, or anus. This can cause a blockage of the chick's normal bowel functions and can lead to death. It happens when chicks are kept in overcrowded conditions such as transport crates or have gone too long without being cleaned. An incorrect diet may also lead to this. Gently remove the obstruction with a moist rag or sponge. Be careful to only remove debris from the vent area, and not from the belly button, which has a natural scab from where the umbilical cord was attached. You can ensure that the area remains clean by applying a small amount of Vaseline, or if the skin looks red, and you suspect inflammation, you can apply a small amount of antibiotic cream. If the pasted vents occur often, you may need to look at the temperature of the brooder, or the type of feed that you are using.

- **Splayed Legs**

Sadly, this is often seen in chicks. Splayed Legs is often seen when a chick has slipped on a slippery floor or has been born with deformed legs. The chick will struggle to walk and will end up on its belly most of the time. A chick that struggles to walk will suffer dietary upsets and will fall victim to being bullied and pecked by other chickens. There is a home remedy for this, which involves gently taping the legs together with vet wrap to limit the legs' ability to split or separate. If the chick can manage to still get around and eat enough, it may strengthen, and the legs may recover.

- **Scissor Beaks**

Chickens with this rare deformity end up looking like *Edward Scissor-Hands*. The affected chick will have a beak where the bottom and top beak do not line up. Chickens will normally sharpen and shape their beaks on rocks or on the hard surfaces near their perches, but they will be unable to do so with this condition. It means that their beaks will not be cleaned as effectively. If you have the funds and a dear pet chicken that suffers from scissor beak, you may consider a surgical option. However, chickens are resilient, and with a little ingenuity on your part, you can ensure that the chicken still has a full life.

You may need to raise the feed bowls so that this chicken can reach the feed with their tongues, as their beaks can't be used to peck up the feed pellets. A finer feed may be useful for such chickens, and you should take care that they are kept apart from other chickens if they are being bullied. For chicks that suffer severe scissor beaks, you may need to wet their feed to ensure that they can easily eat enough to grow. You should take care though with wet feed that it is kept fresh as wet feeds turn sour quickly and can lead to death among all ages of chickens.

- **Cocci**

Known as Cocci by most chicken owners, Coccidiosis is an intestinal disease that kills the most chicks. It is especially prevalent among brooder chicks. Today, many commercial starter feeds have medicine added to prevent this disease. The disease is mostly caused by chicken droppings getting into their water supply. Chicks are the most susceptible. You should ensure that the brooder is cleaned at least twice a day to remove any droppings and check for signs of diarrhea among your chicks. This is usually a sure sign that one or more of your chicks have contracted the disease. Immediately quarantine the chick as the disease is highly contagious and spreads quickly.

Caring for chicks can be a labor of love, but it certainly is a fulfilling and rewarding endeavor to undertake. Most of their care boils down to keeping their environment clean, ensuring that their water and food supply is clean, and watching that the bullying by other chicks or larger chickens doesn't get out of hand. If you have become adept at raising chicks this might also present a lucrative market for you to explore. Buying eggs to hatch or keeping breeding hens to hatch eggs can provide a steady income with good financial returns.

CHAPTER 9

Making Profits

Chickens are a pleasure to keep, but they can be quite expensive. Especially when they have been ill, or in winter months when they need to eat more. If you don't plan effectively, you could also be stuck with a load of excess chickens that you still need to feed. It can take up to 20 weeks before a hen starts laying eggs, and until then, you will enjoy no financial gain from her. Making a profit from keeping chickens seems most unlikely to the uninitiated. Yet there are many backyard chicken keepers who not only defray their chicken keeping costs, but also manage to turn a profit.

Money, Money, Money

Before deciding on pursuing a career or business sideline in raising chickens you need to be aware of the costs involved, the legal restrictions, and the possible markets that you could explore. The law limits the number of chickens that you can keep in a backyard coop, and most places in the U.S. will not permit more than four hens per coup. If you intend on breeding chickens you need to make sure that you have permits if required and get all of your neighbors on board before you buy 50 chickens.

As with any business, you need to draw up a business plan where you work out your costs for feed, the coop, repairs, medicines for chicks, cost of slaughtering birds, and increased power consumption if you use a warming light or electric brooder. You will need to plan for the legal treatment of dead birds and ensure that you have clients to supply or you could sit with over a hundred chicks all needing care in one go. Ten hens can easily outbreed your capacity or finances in one series of hatchings. So before you see dollar signs and read about amazing get-rich-quickly-selling-eggs blogs, you should be realistic. Through planning, preparation, and sheer determination, it is possible to make a respectable income in the poultry business.

Becoming a Breeder

When considering plunging into becoming a breeder there are a few misconceptions to get right out of the way. A breeder is interested in creating quality genetics that improves their chosen breed of chicken. A well-bred chicken, such as the jet-black Ayam Cemani, sells for upwards of $2,500 per bird, and it is the goal of any respectable breeder. If you are interested in becoming a chicken breeder, you need to research the breed that you are interested in. You will need to find the best genetically balanced pair of hens and a quality rooster to begin with. These birds, like other high-quality animals such as racehorses, come with a full genetic history and registration papers with the American Poultry Association (APA).

Being a breeder can be a costly exercise, will require more advanced knowledge about chicken keeping, and is not really ideal for a complete novice to the chicken business. This should not deter someone who is passionate about a chicken breed though. To start off, you should attend chicken shows, read up on breeds, and find out about the different breeders that specialize in the breed that you are interested in. Finding a mentor to help you navigate the foreign waters of being a breeder is an excellent idea. They will help you learn about what makes an excellent specimen in your chosen breed and help you choose a good start off pair.

With any breeders association, there will be some basic rules that the registered breeders will have to adhere to. These could involve the number of chickens that you may breed in a year, the standards under which the birds are to be kept, and of course, there may be fees involved as well as a minimum number of shows that you should attend a year.

Though this may not necessarily put money back in your purse, you can certainly look for sponsors once you are established in the breeding world. However, if it is money that you want to make, then you should look at starting your own hatchery.

A hatchery does exactly what it sounds like, they hatch chicks. This means that you will hatch chicks from fertilized eggs that you buy or alternatively from your own collection of hens. Removing fertile eggs from the nest, will encourage the hen to keep laying for longer, thus producing more eggs.

To start a hatchery, you will need to purchase high-quality hatching equipment such as an electric brooding machine or egg incubator. Many of the companies selling hatching equipment will also help by providing you with knowledge of how to successfully hatch chicks and how to care for them once they have hatched.

Of course, you will need to find a stable market for hatchlings. Thanks to the Internet, you can sell your day-old chicks online by selling them to "factory farms" and also to the general public. There is a thriving market for this and the money is good. On the downside, you will need to consider the expense of buying the equipment, the increased power layout, and multiple chick deaths. This means that you will need to be prepared to dispose of dead chicks in a legally appropriate manner. With power outages in some states due to increased demand in winter, you may also need to invest in a generator to help keep your machines running as even an hour without power can lead to dozens of chicks dying. You will also require a large coop for chicks that have grown too old to sell via the mail, and this will also need to be kept warm with brooding lights, which could again mean more costs as they will need to be fed and monitored regularly. It is not an easy business plan, and it can be quite labor-intensive.

As with any business, you will have to plan carefully, but once you have the basics down, you will be able to run a very lucrative business selling hatchlings.

Selling Eggs

Many backyard chicken owners sell excess eggs to friends and neighbors. This may not necessarily make them millionaires overnight, but it certainly helps to pay for chicken feed and repair costs that are always involved in keeping chickens. Regularly raised chicken eggs can sell for between $3.50 to $5.00 per dozen. Fertilized eggs can also be sold online for as much as $4 an egg, making this quite a viable income. However, if you are serious about selling in bulk you will need to be aware of a few points.

You need to be legal. This may mean getting approval from and setting up a USDA-inspected egg washing facility. It can be costly and will mean that you need to meet certain industry standards. There may also be prohibitions against being an egg seller in the state that you live in. You will need to check on the local laws and municipal bylaws and ordinances to be on the safe side. Remember that to supply large quantities of eggs you will need to keep at least 20 to 50 hens, with young pullets being reared to egg-laying age as well. This will far exceed the local permitted number of chickens that you can keep in your backyard, and you may have to set up shop outside city limits to get around the laws.

Even if you are starting small, it is advisable to write a business plan (Arcuri, 2019). This will help you factor in the costs (buying pullets, feeding, medicines, packaging materials, and transportation) so that you can determine if the local market can support this business. Your market could include local stores, farmers' markets, advertising in local Facebook groups and finding exclusive hotels that want to serve their guests the best. The good thing is that most of your clients will be repeat business, and word of mouth advertising will do the rest. As long as you can ensure availability and quality, you should do very well selling eggs.

Selling Manure

Chickens have several handy products that they produce, and though you may instantly think of eggs and meat, you should also consider selling manure. Chicken manure is in high demand. It makes an excellent fertilizer, and you will find ready markets among gardening enthusiasts, local smallholding farmers, gardening services, and even your local government's offices. Basically anyone who wants to green up their garden, lawn or those who keep vegetable gardens. The good news is that your chickens will supply vast quantities of manure without much work from you. All that is required is that you clean the coops regularly and collect the manure.

However, as with all things that could perhaps affect public health, you will need to consult your local laws to see what is dictated regarding the sale of manure, and the standards under which it should be stored, packed, and transported. Most states require chicken manure to be kept in the shade and for it to be covered at all times with a sheet to minimize the fly load.

Packing the manure into bags will make the handling easier, though you need to factor in the cost of bags. You should also follow good hygiene standards and wear rubber gloves when handling manure and the packed bags of manure. Manure sales may also be seasonal, as people are less likely to buy fertilizer in winter months. This would mean that you need to find an alternative way to dispose of extra manure. To clean out stocks and maintain a good image with the local public, you may want to donate your excess manure to charitable institutions that run vegetable gardens, or old age homes that have ornamental gardens that need fertilizing a few weeks before the winter sets in.

When determining a price for your manure, you should consider other organic fertilizers on the market and price your bags accordingly. You may even find a niche market with organic food producers in your area, though they may have strict requirements as to what you may feed your chickens. Still, considering that manure is a waste product, you can certainly look into selling it to pay for the next month's feed bill.

Selling Hatchlings, Chicks, and Young Chickens

There is a huge market for selling hatchlings, chicks, and young chickens. In the section on becoming a breeder we also looked at starting a hatchery, which sells day-old chicks. The problem with day-old chicks is that the mortality rate is relatively high, and many buyers prefer to buy an older, more robust and lower maintenance chick. The market for pullets is demanding and fast-paced. Many backyard chicken operations and full-time chicken farms are always looking for pullets to replace older hens that are no longer laying as many eggs.

Specializing in pullets would mean that you need to set up your own breeding department, where you select chicks to raise by gender typing them. Pullets sell for $10 to $25 each, however, the demand for roosters is quite low, and this would present a really troubling side to your business. What do you do with chicks that are clearly roosters? Raising them means feeding them, which means spending money. Certainly, some roosters are needed by those wanting to breed their own chickens, but this is a small amount compared to the number of rooster chicks that you would end up with. Roosters also do not make good birds for slaughter, so you might have to destroy chicks that are roosters. Before starting this type of chicken business, you need to decide if this is something that you can accept.

If you are convinced that you will cope with the demands of such a chicken raising business, you have access to a wide market that can indeed make you a huge amount of money if you run the business responsibly. Chicks are hatched within 21 days, so your hens can supply you with a steady stream of hatchlings as you raise the chicks to different ages. Selling chicks that are six weeks old is quite lucrative as many buyers prefer a chick that no longer requires artificial heating. This saves the buyer from the costs of owning their own heating equipment such as electric brooders.

Selling Birds for Slaughter

This side of the poultry industry requires that you either raise your own chicks to a suitable size and age for slaughter or buy pullets that can be reared for slaughter. Again, roosters are not the preferred bird for slaughter.

Hens have more succulent meat and tend to have more meat as a whole. Your feed bill will be quite substantial in this type of business as you are feeding the chickens to gain mass. Having more chickens than the usual maximum on your property means that you need to consult the laws for your area and make applications to the relevant authorities if necessary. You should be prepared for regular and sometimes unannounced inspections to your property when you raise chickens for slaughter. This is to check on the humane conditions under which the birds are raised and also as a matter of public health.

Most large scale businesses that raise chickens for slaughter are located outside of city limits. However, you can target a niche market by providing organically fed and free-ranging chickens to luxury establishments and discerning buyers that will pay a premium to get the best. In this case, you need to ensure quality meat by feeding the best organic feeds, which can cost quite a bit. There are, however, many backyard chicken businesses that make a good side income by selling their excess birds in this way. It is a logical way to replace aged hens with new stock, while making an easy buck.

Again, consider the local laws applicable to slaughtering birds, if you plan on doing the slaughtering yourself. Otherwise, you may need to take the chickens to a registered slaughterhouse to slaughter, cut, and pack the birds for your clients.

Chickens can be a great financial lay-out, when one considers the costs involved in setting up your operation, feeding them, buying equipment, and the sheer amount of time that will go into running things. However, the chickens are not shy about doing their part and will happily provide you with a range of products that you can sell, whether that be eggs, chicks, older pullets, hens for slaughter, and even manure. There is even a limited market for feathers, if you have the time to collect these when your chickens molt. With careful planning and preparation chickens will not only sustain your family, but they may even help your family start a very successful business.

CHAPTER 10

Inside the Mind of a Chicken

Size-wise, a chicken has a really small brain. It's not much bigger than a large peanut, yet it hosts a very active and dynamic mind that is responsible for all of the chicken's behavior. Chickens can be loving, nurturing, protective, affectionate, and then suddenly become vicious and even kill their own kind. Understanding what goes on in a chicken's mind will help you keep the peace in your coop and ensure that your chickens can live in harmony without too much squawking and fuss.

Chicken Psychology 101

As mentioned in chapter five, different breeds of chickens will be known for different temperaments and natures. While most chickens are curious by nature, they also tend to be flighty. Some are very nervous and this then results in either fight or flight. Whatever your chicken is doing, chances are that they are working according to the overarching principle that guides chicken behavior–the pecking order.

Chickens may be domesticated, and they may indeed be cute and fluffy, but there is a reason that their body shapes are reminiscent of the dinosaurs, specifically the T-rex. They can be extremely ferocious, and they will fight for dominion in the flock. Only once all the chickens know where they stand in the order of the flock will they live in relative harmony. Whenever a new chicken gets introduced, the predatory instinct is awakened in the flock, and they will turn to bullying the newcomer. Hens will also be quite merciless in their aggression to the chicks of another hen. They may even go as far as breaking open and eating the eggs of an unattended nest.

When the environment and the necessary resources are limited, your chickens will squabble much more and there will be many more pecking related injuries. If they do not have sufficient space to move around in and respect each other's "territories," your chickens will fight until they have established their own sense of order. This is one of the reasons that you need to ensure that a coop contains at least the minimum space per chicken.

Deviant Behavior

Most chicken dominance or pecking order assertions are quite harmless, however, when a chicken starts to behave in a way that is not suited to the realm of chicken behaviors, we can say that this is deviant behavior. We have already mentioned egg eating as an example of deviant behavior. This can be driven by a calcium deficiency, but usually, it is a result of not receiving enough feed or boredom. Small coops and lack of turn-out in areas where chickens can scratch and be a chicken will cause deviant behaviors.

Chickens will even resort to pecking and pulling out feathers from themselves or other chickens in what may seem like fits of madness. Chances are that the root cause of this is insufficient resources, malnutrition, a lack of an essential vitamin or mineral in their diet, or even the presence of parasites. Boredom and overcrowding is often also a factor. You could consider adding some toys or new elements to the coop such as placing a cabbage head on a string for the chickens to play with.

When a rooster becomes particularly cocky, he may show extreme aggression to the rest of the flock and may over-mate with the hens, actually damaging them with his spurs. This can also be an issue when there are too many roosters with the flock for the available hens. It is not uncommon for roosters in such a situation to "gang-rape" the hens, which can seriously injure the hens. This aggression may even turn against humans, and it can become really dangerous, especially when you are facing a large 4-pound rooster armed with razor-sharp spurs. The only remedy would then be to cull some roosters to restore the natural balance.

Another slightly odd behavior that is more a nuisance than dangerous, is when an older hen starts crowing. This is not all that common, and it usually happens when the rooster has been removed from the flock, leaving only hens.

Aggression and Cannibalism

Chickens can be aggressive towards each other while they establish their pecking order. This pecking order also changes as the different individuals in the flock age and mature. You can see this with young chicks that mock-fight and lightly peck at each other. In a closed environment, this can get out of hand. Considering that chickens are attracted to spots of blood, it comes as no surprise that they will quite easily engage in cannibalism. Chickens do eat their own. Many chicken keepers will even toss chicken bones from slaughtered birds as a source of protein for the rest of the flock. This may not be the safest practice as it may foster cannibalism and lead to diseases. Once a chicken has developed a taste for eggs or the flesh of their own kind, there really isn't much that you can do to help them unlearn it. In severe cases, this may lead to increased fighting and pecking within the flock. You would then have to isolate or slaughter the deviant bird to preserve the integrity and safety of your flock. Cannibalism can be rife among flocks where there is limited space and a lack of good management practices. This is one of the reasons why an injured bird should always be removed from the flock and only returned once it has healed completely.

Flock Behavior

The chicken flock has some very unique and interesting behavior that is quite normal for them to engage in. Briefly speaking, you can expect to see the following behaviors among your flock:

Mock-fighting to moderate fighting: This happens especially among young roosters to find out who's the boss. Usually, it doesn't get too serious, but in an overcrowded coop, this can end in death.

Mating: Young cockerels and pullets mating may seem quite aggressive with the hen protesting loudly and even trying to escape. This is quite normal, however, when there are too many young roosters around, the hens can be injured. Older roosters will sometimes perform a little "dance" in which they drag their wing slightly as they approach the hen, and an older hen will squat down, accepting the rooster's advances.

Crowing roosters: Roosters crow whenever they feel like it. This does not only happen at dawn, unlike what the cartoons would have us believe. They may even crow during the night, which is probably why many cities don't allow the keeping of these loudly calling boys.

Sunbathing: Chickens will sometimes seem as if they have had a stroke and died as they will lie down at an awkward angle with one wing stretched open. This is quite normal as they sunbathe. It may be followed by a dust bath where they will then seem as if they are burying themselves in the sand.

Chicken Calls

Chickens have a range of distinct calls that have different meanings. According to Flip Flop Ranch (2019), chickens have 26 different calls. These can even be combined to create what seems like full sentences as your chickens sit there clucking, cooing, and trilling at each other and at you.

There is a uniquely joyful clucking that a hen makes when she has laid an egg. This may be changed later to a disgruntled squawk as you remove the fresh eggs from the nest. Coop chatter is something that chickens will produce when it's early morning or late evening, and is sort of the chicken equivalent to morning-voices among humans–that soft mumble that we engage in when we don't want to wake up the house.

Growls are not something that only dogs do. Hens can also growl. Usually, this happens when a hen is sitting on a clutch of eggs and is brooding possessively. Trying to move her from her task will result in a warning growl that may send you running.

Groans are often heard when you are petting a particularly tame chicken. It seems to indicate their sheer pleasure at being stroked and held.

Chickens can sound the alarm as they feel threatened, concerned about a new area, or due to an invader in their area. This is a real ruckus with continued shouting from the chickens to warn the rest of the flock. This behavior is usually accompanied by a heightened state of alert in the birds as they swivel their heads around to scope for the item that alerted the first chicken.

One of the most obvious sounds is that made by a mamma hen that has just discovered a tasty morsel for her chicks to enjoy. She will call them closer as she helps them decide what is good to eat and what should be left alone.

Raising chickens may mean that you need to step into the minds of the flock to ensure that they are calm, feel safe, and keep to normal behavior. As long as you respect their need for space and understand their pecking order, your flock will thrive.

CONCLUSION

Raising chickens in your own backyard is a wonderful opportunity to draw your family closer together. It presents a way to teach life lessons to your children in a more organic way, and once a pet chicken has strolled into your heart you will fall head over heels for all things chicken.

With the knowledge that you have gained from this book, you will be well equipped to go out and prepare your backyard to receive your first chickens. You have learned how to choose them, house them, feed them, and take care of them when they are ill. You may even decide to take on a side business to help your hobby pay for itself. However, don't be surprised if your flock of five soon becomes a flock of ten and so on.

Fortunately, chickens are really the gift that keeps on giving. They will allow your family to practice sustainable living, and you can also enjoy farm-fresh organic eggs daily and succulent feasts when you decide to slaughter extra birds. They will bring you closer to nature, and you will probably start a veggie garden, if for no other reason than to give the chickens something to scratch in. Chickens really are a bridge between modern living and farm life for those of us who can't afford to live on a farm.

They are an effective instrument to teach your children responsibility, and can even become emotional support animals. Given their quirky personalities, easy tamability, and busy natures, they offer a distraction to people who are suffering from Post Traumatic Stress Disorder (PTSD), who enjoy the birds nesting on their laps.

Creating a chicken coop and planning a chicken run can be a fun and creative activity that could involve the whole family, which might be the start of the family's bonding experience in raising chickens. Caring for baby chicks, or treating a sick or injured bird may help your children develop and improve their sense of responsibility and emotional intelligence.

While offering all of this to your family, k
own chickens also contributes to their physica
with more nutritious food in the form of fresh eggs and
organic meat. The exercise that you'll get from chasing
the occasional chicken to clean the coop will do wonders
for your heart and bring a smile to your face, not to
mention the excitement of waiting for those first eggs to
hatch, or fetching warm eggs for breakfast.

Having read this book you now know what to feed
your chickens, which kitchen leftovers are safe, and what
to avoid giving your chickens. This will take some of the
guesswork and worry out of keeping your chickens
healthy and productive. Should the worst happen, you also
now know how to deal with chickens that have died, as
well as how to keep your pets or side business legal.

Finally, in this busy and costly world that we live in,
you now have several ways to supplement your income
and improve life for your family through raising chickens.
Whether you simply keep them to supply your own needs,
sell eggs, hatch eggs, raise chicks, breed high-quality
birds, or sell birds for slaughter, chickens certainly offer
dozens of ways in which to make money.

They are fun, entertaining, and clever!

Raising your own chickens will guarantee many an afternoon spent watching them preen and scratch, dust bathe and perch as they become a part of your lifestyle. As Martha Steward pointed out, chickens are indeed interesting additions, and you may become quite attached to having them share your life.

As A Token
of My Gratitude...
Get this FREE guide now!

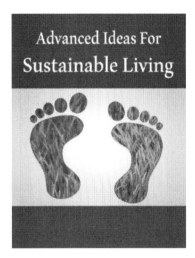

When it comes to sustainability there is a balance. Most people want to do more to live an eco-friendly life, but they also want to make sure that it doesn't consume all of their time, energy, and money.

So how do you know where that balance is? How do you know if you're doing as much as you can do without dramatically changing the way you live your life?

Are You Ready to Take Sustainability to the Next Level?

Are You Ready for a Change?

Are You Looking to Feel More Fulfilled, Rewarded, and Engaged?

If you answered yes to any of these questions then you're ready to take sustainability to the next level. Don't worry; you don't have to go off the grid if you don't want to. Download this free book and you'll learn 8 different ideas to add more sustainable habits and projects to your life. Choose one or all eight – it's up to you. Visit the link below to download:

https://selfempowermentteam.com/sustainable-living

REFERENCES

Arcuri, L. (2019). How to Start an Egg Business. Retrieved from https://www.thespruce.com/start-an-egg-business-3016906

Damerow, G. (2016). Bird Flu and Backyard Chickens: What's the Risk? Retrieved from https://www.storey.com/article/bird-flu-and-backyard-chickens-whats-the-risk/

Flip Flop Ranch. (2019). 26 Sounds That Chickens Make and What They Mean. Retrieved from https://flipflopranch.com/chicken-talk/

4-H Virtual Farm. Chick Embryo Development. Retrieved from https://www.sites.ext.vt.edu/virtualfarm/poultry/poultry_development.html

Jacob, J. (n.d.). Normal Behaviors of Chickens in Small and Backyard Poultry Flocks. Retrieved from https://poultry.extension.org/articles/poultry-behavior/normal-behaviors-of-chickens-in-small-and-backyard-poultry-flocks/

Kelly. (2012). Pros and Cons of Backyard Chickens. Retrieved from https://onceamonthmeals.com/blog/series/get-real/pros-and-cons-of-backyard-chickens/

Lakeside Feeds. (2019). Common Chick Diseases to Look Out For. Retrieved from https://lakesidefeed.com/blog/47506/common-chick-diseases-to-look-out-for

Leonard, J. (2019). 20 Convincing Reasons to Keep Backyard Chickens. Retrieved from https://www.naturallivingideas.com/20-convincing-reasons-to-keep-backyard-chickens/

McGruther, J. (2019). Six Reasons to Keep Chickens. Retrieved from https://nourishedkitchen.com/reasons-to-keep-chickens/

Mormino, K.S. (n.d.). How to Care for an Injured Chicken. Retrieved from https://the-chicken-chick.com/how-to-care-for-injured-chicken-and/

Smith, K. (2014). What Is Sustainable Living? Retrieved
from
https://www.backyardchickencoops.com.au/blogs/lear
ning-centre/what-is-sustainable-living

The Happy Chicken Coop. (2019). The A-Z of Chicken
Breeds and Choosing the Perfect One. Retrieved from
https://www.thehappychickencoop.com/chicken-
breeds/

The Happy Chicken Coop. (2015). 7 Surprising Rules for
Feeding Chickens. Retrieved from
https://www.thehappychickencoop.com/7-surprising-
rules-for-feeding-chickens/

The Happy Chicken Coop. (2018). The Definitive List of
Chicken Treats: What Can Chickens Eat? Retrieved
from https://www.thehappychickencoop.com/chicken-
treats/

Vision Times. (2019). Will Natural Resources Run Out
During Our Lifetime? Retrieved from
http://www.visiontimes.com/2019/08/09/will-natural-
resources-run-out-during-our-lifetime.html

Wikipedia. (n.d.). Chicken manure. Retrieved from
https://en.wikipedia.org/wiki/Chicken_manure

Printed in Poland
by Amazon Fulfillment
Poland Sp. z o.o., Wrocław

58163341R00101